Stand-by Camera One

Love, friendship, and local TV news in 1980

By Steve Newvine

Also by Steve Newvine:

-California Back Roads, Stories from the Land of the Palm & Pine
-Growing Up Upstate, Memories from the 1960s and 70s
-Grown Up, Going Home, Reconnecting with Port Leyden
-Soft Skills for Hard Times (Self help)
-Sign Off at Sunrise (Novel)
-Ten Minutes to Air (A murder mystery)
-Go Where You're Needed, (Holiday short story)
-Microphones, Moon Rocks, and Memories- Selected Columns
-Friend Through the End, Reflections on Family, Friends,& Fairways
-Finding Bill, A Nephew's Search for Meaning

Available at Lulu.com , Amazon, and BN.com

ISBN: 978-0-359-23519-3

No part of this book can be used, duplicated, translated, or presented by any means including print, audio, or digital without the expressed written consent of the author.

Copyright 2018 by Steve Newvine

Stand-by Camera One

Love, friendship, and local TV news in 1980

By Steve Newvine

Chapters

Introduction	6
Prologue	9
When Can You Start	11
Stand by Camera One	16
Peace Begins in the Parking Lot	21
Triple Cities People	31
Andy	35
The Ring is Under the Beer Can	40
Continuous Improvement	43
The Big Day	51
An Offer	59
Moving On	63
Farewell My Friend	68
Leaving Town	71
Settled In	74
Epilogue	76
Bonus- Columns/Book Excerpt	81
Pictures	95
Recipie	99

Dedicated to three people who played such important roles in my first eighteen months on the job in Binghamton.

To Mark, thanks for hiring me.

To Vaune, thanks for marrying me.

To Andy, thanks for stressing that life is like a game of chess: it helps to plan your next move, and the move after that one, and the move after that.

Introduction

Three significant events happened in the seventeen months following my graduation from Syracuse University in May 1979. Those events were: landing my first job as a television news reporter, the friendship with a chess player who helped shape my adult life, and the marriage to my soulmate Vaune.

This all happened in the southern tier of upstate New York in a region best known as the Triple Cities. The Triple Cities are Binghamton, Endicott, and Johnson City.

Binghamton is the largest of the Triple Cities with a population of 47,376 (2010 census, Broome County population: 200,600). Endicott and Johnson City are officially villages, but that didn't stop whoever coined the phrase Triple Cities. Both villages owe their existence to Mr. Henry Bradford Endicott and Mr. George F. Johnson, who created the shoe manufacturing enterprise that would become the Endicott-Johnson Shoe Company.

A first job, a friendship, and a marriage. These three significant life events are not necessarily unique. We all remember our first full-time job in our chosen field. How could anyone forget a special friend who came into your life in adulthood and who, in turn, became a standard bearer for the values that define the person you are. Becoming engaged and getting married defies explanation. It is an extraordinary experience.

In this book, three stories are interwoven in the backdrop of the Triple Cities. This is my story of a very special time.

I'll also share some significant news and sports events that happened during that seventeen month period. The "news briefs" appearing at the beginning of each chapter are what a news anchor or sportscaster might have read on that day's newscast. I hope this creates a timeline of what was going on in the world while I was proceeding along my career and life pathways. If you're old enough, I hope the TV news leads bring back some memories.

My professional career began one week before the Memorial Day holiday at the studio of station WICZ-TV on the Vestal Parkway in Binghamton. Just two weeks prior, I interviewed for the job during a break in my final examinations at Syracuse University. A few days after the interview, you would find me cheering at the Manley Field House at SU when my school, the S. I. Newhouse School of Public Communications, was announced by Chancellor Melvin Eggers.

Hearing the name of my school within Syracuse University announced from the podium was my personal graduation ceremony. The graduating class was too big to read each graduate's name publically, let alone having each graduate march across the stage to accept a diploma.

NBC News Anchor Tom Brokaw, a *Today Show* star in 1980, gave the commencement address. There wasn't anything memorable from his speech, although a clipping saved from a local newspaper did reference Brokaw urging graduates to take chances and ask the tough questions. I do recall how he made light of a sign some graduates held up that asked "where's Jane Pauley." Tom pointed out the sign, and then told the audience that the sign-maker had misspelled his *Today Show* co-anchor's last name.

Following the commencement ceremony, my family and my girlfriend Vaune posed for pictures, met my friends and some of the parents of my friends, and said our goodbyes. My family headed back about an hour-and-a-half north to Port Leyden, where my parents were planning a party in my honor to be held the next day. I spent the afternoon at Green Lakes State Park outside Syracuse with Vaune. She would later head to Alfred in western New York for her brother's college graduation ceremony that would take place the next day.

My Bachelors in Arts diploma was shipped to my parents' home about two months after the ceremony. By then, I was already working as a reporter at WICZ-TV, Channel 40, in Binghamton.

As the late radio commentator Paul Harvey would say, here's the rest of the story.

Prologue

January 20, 1980

My wife of six months is sitting beside me on the couch. It's a day off from my new job as weekend co-anchor and reporter for station WAAY-TV in Huntsville, Alabama.

We are watching television where the inauguration of Ronald Reagan is taking place in Washington, DC. But we also have our eyes on another story.

On the other side of the globe, freedom is moments away for the American hostages held in Iran since November 1979.

A day in the television news business doesn't get much better than this: two major stories unfolding at the same time. But I'm not working in the newsroom. Weekend co-anchors get their days off during the week. So whether I like it or not, I'm observing this confluence of two major stories from my living room. But I don't mind. It's an amazing time in history and we're totally focused on watching it unfold before us on our Sylvania twenty-inch color television; a wedding gift from my parents.

It's hard to believe that in the past year-and-a-half, so much has changed in our lives. In May 1979, I started my first job in television news. Fourteen months later, Vaune and I were married. In between, a friend who made a tremendous impact on me came into my life.

> "To protect and defend the constitution of the United States, so help me God."

The final words of the oath of office are repeated by Ronald Reagan. The President is sworn in, the inauguration speech is well received, a parade down Pennsylvania Avenue celebrates the start of a new administration, a former President leaves the nation's capital heading home to Georgia, and word is received that the airplane carrying the hostages has cleared Iranian air space.

As these events are playing out before my eyes on the television screen, I can't help but think about the whirlwind that has been my life for the past eighteen months.

Chapter 1- When Can You Start? Monday!

May 21, 1979 Newscast- "The verdict is guilty for former San Francisco City Councilman Dan White. He was convicted today of manslaughter in last year's shooting of Mayor George Moscone and Councilman Harvey Milk."

I wanted to be on television since elementary school.

We lived on the same street as Port Leyden Central School in upstate New York. My older brother Terry and I would walk to school every day. When my sister Becky started school, the three of us would walk together down the street and through the Lincoln Street entrance of the school.

Most days, we'd walk home for lunch. Mom would always have it ready. We'd eat, and then head back for playground time before the afternoon session. We didn't go home every day for lunch, but when we did, it was special.

I'm not sure whether this is actually true or just my perception, but it seems to me that I went home for lunch more often than my siblings. Part of the reason for this was the home cooked meal Mom would prepare. The other part was the NBC game show *Concentration*. Watching Hugh Downs host, I'd play along with the two contestants who would match prizes and solve the puzzle.

Before long, I got a *Concentration* home game. With my toy wooden blocks, and the home version's puzzle board, I'd stage the game show set and replay that day's broadcast when I arrived home from school in the afternoon.

Another favorite of mine was host Bill Cullen. He was the master of ceremonies for the original *Price is Right*. Mom would tell stories of how as a preschooler, I would use my bathrobe as a sport coat, pretend I was Bill Cullen, and make believe I was a game show host.

I grew out of those pretend television hosting days and became a fan of daytime talk shows as I moved into my middle-school years. *The Mike Douglas Show* aired on station WKTV in Utica every afternoon beginning at 4:30. As I got a little older, I made a deal with my mom to allow my watching of the *Tonight Show Starring Johnny Carson* on Friday nights and during school vacations.

In high school, we all were sort of forced to figure out what we wanted to do with our lives after graduation. I chose the Radio/TV Broadcasting program at Herkimer County Community College (now known as Herkimer College).

In my senior year at South Lewis Junior/Senior High School, I got a letter that put me on the track to work in broadcasting.

The letter was in response to an inquiry I made to our local radio station WBRV in Boonville, New York about doing a weekly school news report over the airwaves. The person who had previously done the job had graduated from high school.

In the letter, the station's news director invited me to set up a time for a voice audition. I promptly called the station, set up an appointment, auditioned, was reminded it did not pay anything, and got the job.

It was the first real-world step in my broadcasting career.

While reporting school news in my senior year of high school did not produce income, the experience paid off about seven months after graduation. By then, I was in the Radio/TV program at Herkimer. The Boonville radio station was in need of a weekend announcer. During one of my college breaks, I paid a visit to the weekday morning announcer, a man by the name of George Capron. George played my taped school news reports on the air the previous year. I guess that visit kept my name alive when the part-time opening came up.

George suggested the station manager give me a call. Thanks to my recent successful test for a Federal Communications Commission Broadcast License, I got the gig.

After landing that weekend announcer job, the outlook for a planned career in broadcasting looked promising. Now, just a few months after starting college, here was a job in the field where I was pursuing my degree.

Between records on the air, I read announcements for lost pets, weather reports warning of pending snow storms, and generally kept company with my small audience in rural upstate New York.

In my final semester at Syracuse University, I secured a television news internship at station WKTV in Utica. The college class schedule permitted me flexibility so that I could make the one-hundred mile round trip drive from my college dormitory to the station three days a week. I have always been indebted to news director Jack Durant for approving the internship and giving me the opportunity to do on-air reporting. I also worked with great teachers such as reporter Bill Carroll, anchor Bill Worden, and weatherman Lyle Bosely.

By the end of the internship, I was filing on-air reports. Those stories helped make up an audition tape to show potential employers.

A copy of that audition tape caught the eye of Mark Williams, the news director at WICZ-TV in Binghamton, New York. The news director is the department head for a broadcast newsroom.

I interviewed during the finals week at Syracuse. While I was in Binghamton, I stopped by the studios of WMGC channel thirty-four to drop off my resume and see if I could talk to their news director.

The receptionist at WMGC took my resume and asked me to wait as she left the front office. Within minutes, she returned to escort me to the station manager's office.

I met with a man named Phil Marella who extended the courtesy of an informational interview. He had no openings, but he encouraged me to remain diligent and to check with him from time to time. We parted with my full knowledge that now I have a friend in the Binghamton media market.

Back at WICZ, Mark called me a few days later to say I was still in the running to fill the reporter role at the station, but he had to run everything past his station manager before making it official.

My elation transitioned to worry a few days later. I wondered whether my interview for the job at WICZ was enough to take me to the finish line. I wanted to write or call the station's general manager to make my case, but I did not want the idea to backfire and maybe offend the news director.

Taking Phil up on his offer to stay in touch, I called him. I told him what I was thinking and he gave me some sound advice.

"Write the letter to the station manager, but CC the news director so that you keep everything out in the open," he said.

I thanked him and quickly mailed a brief letter to the WICZ station manager with the carbon copy going to Mark.

About a week later, Mark from called me on a Thursday night to give me a final interview over the phone. After about a half hour, he said I was his choice, but that he'd have to run everything past the Station Manager. He said he'd call the next day.

I hardly slept that night. I was worried about whether there might be some bit of hesitation on the Station Manager's part. The next day, I stayed close to the phone. By 6:30 that night, I braced myself for what might be a long weekend. Then the phone rang.

Mark made the formal offer. I accepted immediately.

"When can you start?" he asked.

"How about Monday?" I answered.

That weekend, I packed up what I needed to get started in my new city. By Sunday, I was scouring the local newspaper looking for apartments for rent. I found one in Johnson City that was close to work. The landlord let me move in that day. I slept on a cot that I borrowed from someone I knew.

I was ready to go to work the next day.

Chapter 2- Stand-by Camera One

May 21, 1979 Sportscast "The Islanders will face the Canadiens tonight for game five of the Stanley Cup Play-offs. Montreal holds a 3-1 lead in the best of seven series.

I walked into the lobby of WICZ-TV, channel forty, shortly before noon on May 21, 1979. I told the receptionist who I was and she called the newsroom. Two minutes later, Mark Williams greeted me.

We walked through the studio and made our way to the small newsroom. From there, Mark turned up the sound of a twelve-inch black and white television set that rested on top of a four-drawer filing cabinet. The noon newscast from competitor WBNG-TV channel twelve was just coming on the air. Mark watched the first segment of the newscast with a pen and pad in his hands to jot down any story subjects that he felt might be worth following up on for that night's six o'clock news.

I had seen this newsroom before during my job interview. It had three large metal desks with chairs, a four-by-six foot work table, the four-drawer filing cabinet, and a small typewriter stand behind the news director's desk. A police scanner was picking up calls on the various radio frequencies tuned into the device.

Each desk had a *Smith-Corona* electric typewriter. Some of my classmates in college had similar models. The typewriter's had removable cartridges for typewriter ribbon. The news director's desk sat at the far end of the newsroom. My desk would be in the middle. The last desk was for the part time reporter who was covering news in the morning. It would eventually become the desk for the next full time person hired to work in the news department.

Missing from what looked like an ordinary television newsroom in the late 1970s small market station was the presence of a teletype machine. The news budget was so small at WICZ, the station did not subscribe to a wire service like Associated Press or United Press International. The "tick-tick" sound of a press wire was common in most broadcast stations. That would not be the case here.

WICZ programmed a half-hour of local news Monday-Friday at six and eleven PM. The station also did two five-minute newscasts that ran during the local breaks of NBC's *Today Show* at 7:25 and 8:25 AM. While we did not talk about it either in my job interview or even now on my first day, the station hoped to program news seven-days a week sometime in the future.

At about ten minutes after twelve o'clock, Mark turned the television set volume down, grabbed his keys, and tested the beeper attached to the side of his belt.

"Come on," he said with a smile. "Let's go to lunch."

We headed to a nice restaurant in the Vestal Plaza and enjoyed a buffet lunch. When he hired me, Mark said to plan on lunch with him on the first day. It was his way of getting our working relationship off to a good start. When the check arrived, I reached for my wallet only to be told by Mark. "This one's on me."

I spent the rest of the afternoon meeting the staff at channel forty. I was shown my desk and given what amounted to an employee orientation. Mark reviewed the union contract. My job was classified as an announcer in the union contract between WICZ-TV and the National Association of Broadcast Engineers and Technicians (NABET). I would eventually get my union card. It was my second card as I had to join a meat-cutters union for a part-time grocery store job I held when I was going to college.

It came as no surprise that I would be going on the air that night. Orientation was nice, but baptism by fire was the only way to learn in a small market television station. From my desk in the newsroom, I started preparing a three-minute sports report. With all the journalism training I had at Herkimer College and Syracuse University, I never did anything in the sports reporting arena. This was the local news business, and we were ready to jump in and go to work.

There's a recording in my personal archives of my first broadcast on local television. Mark Williams anchored the station's newscast as well as served as news director. He introduced me to the viewers.

"We welcome Steve Newvine to the Eyewitness News team. Steve has lived upstate all his life and recently graduated from Syracuse. Steve, welcome to the Triple Cities."

I thanked Mark, and began to read a short sports report and an even shorter weather forecast.

Behind the studio wall, the newscast director, Rick Krolak was working the six o'clock newscast. The director controls all the video and audio components that go into a television production. He or she calls for a specific camera shot, a particular source of audio to be opened, or a video tape to be played. In bigger markets, the director would work with a technical director who would run the video switcher that allows takes from one camera to another. At WICZ, both roles were handled by the director using dialogue that would sound a little like this:

> "Stand-by camera one. Take one, ready two. Take two, stand by tape, in three-two-one. Take tape."

From Monday through Thursday between the six and eleven o'clock newscasts, I would attend various government council meetings and prepare a report for the late news.

On Friday, there was no local government meeting. That meant my photographer and I had to enterprise a story. We had to come up with something our viewers might be interested in seeing.

My first enterprise story was about rising gasoline prices. In 1979, gas was selling for ninety-cents a gallon. My photographer was Rick who took the video camera between directing the six and eleven o'clock newscasts and accompanied me to news stories. Rick and I went to a local gas station, interviewed customers pumping gas, and did a "stand-up" close to the package.

Mark and I watched the story as it aired from the studio. I should say Mark watched the story. I watched Mark watch the story. He smiled after it aired.

I made it through my first week on the air as a television news reporter.

In the weeks to come, I'd crank out stories from the various local government council meetings, and mix in stories about things happening in the community.

When the local regatta was held in the early summer, I went out with a photographer on a Sunday to cover the races. This regatta featured decorated rafts cruising down mostly shallow waters in Binghamton. We put together some interviews and highlights and ran packaged reports on Monday's newscasts.

One summer night, we drove past a park where several men were pitching horseshoes. Rick stopped so that I could get out and ask whether this was some sort of special event. The organizer told me it was the weekly horseshoe league. Rick started shooting video as I gathered information about the length of the season, how many men were participating, whether any women were participating (they were not participating in that league back in 1979), and what did the top team stand to win at the end of the season. The result was a neat little package about a pastime that kept of lot of men in the Triple Cities busy during the summer months.

As the report filed on that night's newscast stated, the men finished their league in the fall, right before the start of bowling season.

Rick and I had to work fast. Upon returning to the station, I had to write and narrate the story so that Rick could edit. After the story, I would begin writing that night's sportscast while Rick prepared for his other role as director of the news broadcast.

All of us working on the newscast were great multi-taskers. We had to be in order to survive.

Chapter 3- Peace Begins in the Parking Lot

June 12, 1979 Newscast "With the planned return of what's left to NASA's Skylab space station next month, some folks are having fun at the space agency's expense. In North Carolina, a local hotel designated itself an official Skylab crash zone complete with a painted target in the parking lot."

The summer of 1979 was all about firsts.

I came to Binghamton with one suit and two sport coats. That would take me through three days of local television reporting before having to repeat the cycle. I needed so add to my wardrobe. I bought my first wool suit from a tailor shop in Johnson City that was going out of business. I paid for it with money from my first WICZ paycheck.

Within a couple of months, it was clear that I needed a better set of wheels. With my dad co-signing a loan, I bought my first new vehicle. My 1979 *Toyota* pick-up truck was purchased from a dealer in Endicott. I was slowly contributing to the economy of the Triple Cities.

I also had my first real encounter with covering a weather-related event for television.

On a mid-summer afternoon, torrential rains fell on the Triple Cities after nearly two weeks of drought. The storm hit around 3:30 in the afternoon. Mark and I agreed that we needed to get some video for that day's six o'clock news.

Rick had come in the newsroom to get ready for directing the six o'clock news. Our daytime photographer Peg had already left for the day. Her shift started around 5:30 in the morning and ended around two in the afternoon.

In theory, we did not have anyone to shoot the story. Rick overheard Mark and I discuss how I would shoot the video in a safe way without getting into an accident. Rick, recognizing the potential for a compelling video story, offered to shoot while I would drive through the rain storm.

For about an hour, we made our way through heavy rain, large puddles, and stranded motorists. Our little Mercury Comet news car was seemingly spinning all over the place. Rick kept shooting video while I tried to drive in a straight line.

We got back to the station and Rick quickly edited about ninety seconds of video. Mark narrated what the viewers were seeing almost extemporaneously. I provided some facts, but most of the story was just reporting what the viewer was seeing. The result was truly compelling television for 1979 standards.

After the six o'clock newscast, Rick and I would grab a bite to eat before heading off to a city council or town board meeting. We took in the fast food offerings that were close to where the meetings were being held.

About once a week, the *Binghamton Sun Bulletin* newspaper would run an ad from a local restaurant offering a special on spedies. I asked around and learned that spedies were a local favorite. Pieces of lamb, chicken, and sometimes pork were marinated in a special mixture of oil, vinegar, and spices. The marinated meat was put on skewers and barbecued over charcoal.

To paraphrase one of my favorite sayings, there was nothing wrong in that description. I had to try this.

So one night, Rick and I headed off to that restaurant mentioned in the newspaper ad. It was worth every penny.

I also heard about *Pat Mitchell's Ice Cream*. Made on location from a shop in the village of Endicott, this was another local favorite. We made *Pat Mitchell's* a regular stop any time we were in that part of the viewing area.

Some of those hot summer nights in 1979 were ready-made for *Pat Mitchell's Ice Cream*. Some nights, the line going into the shop was at least fifty to sixty people long. The line moved quickly. It was always worth the wait.

There were other things to experience such as the *Roberson House* on Front Street in Binghamton, the local symphony better known as the *BC Pops* (BC standing for Broome County), and *All Saints Church* off the traffic circle on the Harry L Drive. One of the priests at *All Saints* would end his liturgy with a warning, "Remember, peace begins in the parking lot."

All Saints Church was packed for Midnight Mass at Christmas in 1979. I remember leaving early for church and walking in the crisp Christmas Eve air. I should have left earlier as I ended up standing throughout the service.

There were plenty of good restaurants in the Triple Cities. There's a saying that if you want to find a good place to eat, just look at the parking lot. If you see a lot of trucks in the lot, that's a good barometer that the restaurant is good. I'd add to that by saying if you see a local news team car in the lot, there's a good chance you have found an excellent place to eat.

For fancy dining, my favorite place in the twin tiers was *O'Briens* in Waverly. A driver could see the huge sign for *O'Briens* from highway seventeen. The sign looked like how the Hollywood sign is seen in the hills overlooking the entertainment capitol. The view from the dining room took in a wide swath of the southern tier of New York and the northern tier of Pennsylvania.

We had a lot of fun, but we were well aware that our station was at a disadvantage. Channels 2-13 were the original open bands on the television spectrum and were much easier for home antennas to capture in the early decades of television history. Being on the VHF band, with all their competitors on the UHF band, gave WBNG, on channel twelve, a big edge in the 1950s, 60s, and 70s. Consequently, WBNG was able to build up a huge share of the local audience for news.

WBNG had the lead and they were running with it. They had a much larger staff than our team at channel forty. They were the big guns in the market.

Another competitor in the market was public television affiliate WSKG. While they were not competing for ratings like the commercial stations in the market, they were doing a lot of longer packages of five-to-seven minutes in length that were a far stretch from the ninety-second packages we were producing. WSKG also had some of the best field equipment for that time in local news.

There was a new feeling in the management ranks that the station could make a dent in channel twelve's dominance. WICZ hired Sal Anthony about two months after I started. Sal was working at a station in Bluefield, West Virginia. At our station, he would do sports on the six and eleven newscasts as well as cover night meetings and spot news as needed. As part of Mark's plan to grow the news team, my shift was moved to daytime.

Sal and I were in the same mold of electronic journalist trying to pick up experience with an eye on the future. We both learned from one another. I could handle a heavy writing workload covering about a half-dozen stories a day. Sal had no problem shooting some of his own sports stories if he needed to. Whatever it took to compete against a dominant station with a staff about four times the size as ours, we did it.

Sal also showed me how to tie a perfect Windsor knot in my necktie. His instructions on tie-tying stayed with me throughout my professional life.

Shortly after Sal came on board, the station set up an interview with the *Binghamton Sun Bulletin* about the new emphasis on local news from WICZ. In an article from the August 5, 1979 issue of the *Sun Bulletin*, (*WICZ News is like Avis- Team Strives "Harder" for Number One*) Mark, Sal, and I were asked about our roles in the new look for the station's newscast. Mark said, "There's a new attitude here. Before, news was something that was done to fill FCC (Federal Communications Commission) requirements. Now we're serious about it. We're building an aggressive team."

Sal's comments in the story took a shot at channel twelve. "I don't think WBNG has really had any hard competition before."

My comments were focused on the job I was doing. In a four-hundred word article, I got six words, "We're interested in quality over quantity." While I said a lot more in that reporter's interview with the three of us, I naturally had no control over what he used for my quotes in the article. But that did not matter to me. As I would learn throughout my career dealing with media, less is better.

Our new news team was off and running. But soon, we would encounter our first departure from the ranks. In the fall of 1979, Rick announced that he had been hired by WNEP channel sixteen in Wilkes-Barre, Pennsylvania. Channel sixteen was becoming one of the best news organizations in the northeast. They had a large staff, state of the art *TK-76* field video cameras, and a helicopter. Rick had always wanted to work at a station that had all the tools that television journalists needed. We all wished him well.

Rick's departure happened shortly after I was switched over to a daytime shift. Mark wanted me to be the street reporter covering daily news in and around Binghamton. My photographer on the daytime shift was Peg. We got along well and did our best to cover all the news conferences, political appearances, and spot news like fires and accidents that we could squeeze into our work day.

On a regular day, I would do one or two full package reports and about a half-dozen voice-over stories or voice-over-sound-on-tape interview stories. A package story included my narration and usually a stand-up ending or bridge. The voice-over stories were to be read on the air by the anchor.

A typical dayshift for me started at my apartment with the delivery of the *Binghamton Sun Bulletin*, one of two local daily newspapers published by Gannett. I would read the paper while watching the *Today Show* and the local news updates on my station. After my coffee and cereal, I was ready for my five-minute drive to the station.

The day shift would have this basic itenery: 8:30- arrive at the station, 9:00-2:00- gather stories out in the field (and squeeze in lunch), 2:00-5:30- write stories and do any studio work such as our public affairs segment (called *Close-Up*, more on that later). If I was needed to fill in as evening news or sports anchor, I'd stay later. If there was a news story to cover in the afternoon, I would adjust the rest of the routine in order to accommodate that assignment.

Upon my arrival at the station, I would review what was in the "future file" for that day. A future file at that time was a manila folder with the date of the month written in the tab. Inside the file were news releases, newspaper clippings, and handwritten notes regarding possible story ideas.

News releases tied to a specific date were filed in that date's future file. Clippings were generally considered background information for a possible enterprise story. Notes were usually from Mark with suggestions for possible follow up stories or requests that I check on something either at City Hall or at the County Office Building. On most days, Mark would call me at the station with ideas he developed overnight.

After reviewing everything, I would work out a schedule for our time in the field.

Our first stop on most days was at the Government Complex in downtown Binghamton. This complex had City Hall, the Broome County Government Center, and the New York State Office Building all in the same plaza. We would park our car in a "news media" spot inside the parking structure, and then head up to the Mayor's press room for a daily news conference. I assumed that many years prior to my working in Binghamton, the daily news conference was set up so that the Mayor would not have to do individual interviews with each member of the local media.

The Mayor was available usually two days a week. On the other days, a City department head might show up to promote something going on in their organization. We generally used everything that was covered in the news conference, although it bothered some of us that we relied so heavily on City Hall to provide the source material for their news. In a perfect world, the reporters would be generating most of the ideas for stories. But this was a smaller news market, and each television and radio station had newscasts to fill.

Some of the department heads who filled in on the City Hall daily news conference included the Fire Chief. The Chief was clearly a brave and respected man, but it seemed that to many of us in the local media he was always talking about smoke detectors. No matter where the fire was, or how it was caused, the Chief always seemed to work in how the damage would have been far less had smoke detectors been either installed or were in good working order. The Chief was a visionary. He was talking about smoke detectors long before every public safety official was talking about them.

Twice a week, the County Executive would have a news conference. Usually, that conference was timed with knowledge that most of the local media would be at the City Hall briefing.

We would go to the State Office building either to interview our local Assembly member or State Senator. Our State Senator was Warren Anderson who held the position of Senate Majority Leader. Sometimes, there might be a visit from Albany of the State Attorney General or the Commissioner of the Department of Environmental Conservation. We usually attended some kind of media event in the State Office building once a week. The State Attorney General Robert Abrams would fly in about once every other month to talk about some investigation his office was doing.

I remember one time when Abrams showed up about forty-five minutes late for the news conference and explained he was delayed due to a problem with a commuter airline. We asked him whether his office might investigate that airline, and he said, "Now that you mention it, we might just do that." About two weeks later, he was back in Binghamton to tell the media how his office had launched an investigation into commuter airline service in the state.

The rest of the morning was filled with quick trips to schools, hotels, ribbon cuttings, or any type of manufactured events that the public relations representatives from various organizations might invite us to cover. Sometimes, we might develop a full package report from one of these media events. More often, we would shoot some video and an interview and turn it into a shorter story that the news anchor would voice over (VO in our lingo) the footage leading to a brief sound-on-tape (SOT).

In his off hours, Mark was part of a volunteer ambulance squad. He carried a pager and would often be paged about ambulance calls. The news department had a pager as well. I would carry it during my shift. If Mark heard about an ambulance call or picked up an emergency call from the newsroom police scanner, he'd page and either ask us call the station for details, or just tell us where the accident or fire was. Most of the time, we could pick up the spot news like a fire or an accident. Sometimes, the event was a bust; that was usually good news for the family involved but a challenge for those of us covering several news stories for that night's newscast.

What time remained in our workday was generally spent trying to connect with a potential news interview for either a story related to something we picked up at the news conferences, or a story we developed on our own.

Lunch was usually on the run or we'd grad a sandwich from the deli at the *Grand Union* grocery story in the *Vestal Plaza* near the station. I still remember a special at the *Grand Union* deli of a sandwich on marble bread (rye and pumpernickel) with a small cup of macaroni salad for $1.29.

Peg and I grew weary of the large number of stories we were expected to generate. I had to write them, and Peg had to shoot and edit them. But we both were career conscious and knew that our work would reflect on us while we were at WICZ, and later in our careers if we were to leave the station.

I suggested to Peg that every day, we'd try to focus on at least one story that we could develop into what we called our "quality piece" or "QP". We knew we had to turn out most of the local video stories for that night's six o'clock newscast, but we thought if we could do an exceptional job on just one of those stories, we'd have something we could be proud of in the future. The concept worked so well, that often Peg would whisper to me at a news conference to suggest that maybe the subject of this particular story could be developed into a "QP". After the news conference, we'd start talking about which elements we needed to include, while making sure we picked up enough of the other stories happening around town to help fill the newscast. I'd scramble to write and memorize a "stand-up" that we could shoot to give the package a good conclusion or transition.

Among the QPs Peg and I produced that I still remember was one on contamination of the City of Binghamton water supply. The public works director mentioned in a news conference how levels of a certain toxic chemical had fallen in recent months. We took that tidbit from the news conference, and then headed off to the purification facility to shoot a stand up. I confirmed the public works director's comments with the State of New York and we had a decent story for that night's newscast.

In early August, New York Yankees catcher Thurman Munson died in a plane crash in Ohio. We wondered whether there was a local angle. Peg remembered that Major League Baseball umpire Ron Luciano lived in Endicott. We tracked down his number through a mutual acquaintance. That person took our message, and then contacted Ron. Later that day, we interviewed Ron about his experiences working games behind Munson. We ran that story in both the news and sports segments (in a different format using a different portion of Ron's interview) that night.

We had fun with a story about a woman who created paintings using toilet paper as a brush. This artist had been featured on the NBC television show *Real People*. Peg and I spent some time with the artist as she demonstrated how the work was created. The artist gave me the painting. I held on to it for several years before it was lost during one of my many moves.

Within a few months, both Peg and I produced several stories that we felt were our best quality pieces. I took the best three or four packages and put them on a videotape in the event I might be asked by a news director in another market to send in an audition reel. It felt good to have something ready should I be ready to pitch for a bigger and better opportunity.

But I was in no hurry to leave Binghamton. Not yet.

Chapter 4- Triple Cities People

August 1979 Newscast- "Some colorful language from President Carter regarding a possible primary challenge from Senator Ted Kennedy. Parents may want to send their children into another room for the next twenty-seconds. The President, when asked whether he fears a possible fight for the Democratic Party nomination, told reporters, and we quote: "if Ted Kennedy runs, I'll whip his ass." No comment yet from Senator Kennedy."

I got to meet a lot of people during my time on channel forty. Being a reporter on local television helped break the ice when meeting new people. Many recognized me from the WICZ newscasts. The conversation would usually start with a person asking me, "Are you the guy on the news?"

I remember one night I was taking a walk in Johnson City near highway seventeen. This neighborhood was real close to the four-lane highway, but the people I met did not seem to mind the noise. A man who looked like he was in his sixties saw me walking by.

"Are you the guy on the news?" he asked.

I told him yes, and he started talking to me about everything going on in his life. He introduced me to his next door neighbors and invited me to join him for a beer. I was amazed that I got this kind of attention from a person who only knew me from seeing me on local television.

In the summer of 1979, the station hired a part time person to help cover vacation shifts within the office ranks. Ann Marie grew up in Binghamton, and had just completed her first year studying communications at college. While I had my own work to keep me occupied, I offered her suggestions on the type of classes she should take as electives over the next three years of college. At the end of the summer, her mother and father had me to their home to thank me for helping their daughter learn more about local television. Their family was another example of the kind nature of the people I met in the Southern Tier.

One of my news contacts worked in communications at the local United Way. Our station covered the annual United Way campaign with vigor. We attended the kick-off luncheon, did frequent campaign update stories, and covered the final report luncheon. During one of our interviews, the communications officer told me he was from Utica. As I had done my television internship at WKTV in Utica, we had a connection. We went out to lunch after the campaign had wrapped up.

After a 6:00 o'clock newscast one night, I went into the newsroom to file that night's script in our filing cabinet. The station's shipping manager (who also served as our audio engineer during the newscasts) came into the newsroom to tell me I had a visitor.

My visitor was a friend I met at Herkimer College four years ago. He lived in the Triple Cities all his life. He was a great guy and we performed together in musical productions at the College's *Lyric Theater* group. We lost touch after graduation in 1977. That night, we visited for about a half hour, and unfortunately we never connected after that. The last I heard about him was from a family member who responded to my Facebook inquiry with an update that my friend and his wife are living in Alaska.

One of the radio stations in Binghamton hired a reporter named Lynda from Seneca Falls. I met Lynda at a news conference and she told me she was looking for an apartment. I gave her the name and number of my landlord. She took an apartment in my building.

Lynda also told me when the new Billy Joel album was out in the stores. Billy Joel was a big part of my Syracuse University experience. His album *The Stranger* was playing all the time on the floor at my dorm. Practically everyone from our floor got tickets to see Billy play at the Syracuse War Memorial Auditorium in 1978.

The album was *Glass Houses* and I rushed out to buy it as soon as Lynda told me it was out. The album did not disappoint. Billy's classics such as *It's Still Rock and Roll to Me* and *You May Be Right* were featured on that album.

One Friday night in the summer after I had wrapped up my reporter's shift, I started to head north my parent's house for the weekend. It started to rain and somewhere along the road I saw a man trying to hitch a ride. Even in 1979, the idea of picking up a stranger was not considered smart. But the man looked like he needed to catch a break.

I stopped, rolled down the passenger window, and asked, "Where you heading?"

"Utica, or anyplace near there," was his answer.

I let him in. In 1979, I was more likely to do something like that. I certainly would not do it today.

For the next hour, the man told me how he was hoping to meet a friend at the YMCA in Utica. He was an older man, probably in his fifties. I took the opportunity to learn more about this man's back story. How did he end up hitching a ride on a rainy night north of the Broome County line? I guess I just wasn't that inquisitive. We made small talk, and when we arrived in Utica, I dropped him off on Genesee Street. He thanked me and I wished him well.

Fast forward to Thanksgiving Day in Binghamton. I had to work the daytime shift on what must be the slowest news day of the year. Fred Heckman was my photographer. Fred was a great guy who filled in as a photographer, reporter, and anchor when needed. His regular job was working in the production department producing commercials. Fred told me he worked a lot of holidays over the years and that every year, the station would go to the local Salvation Army and do a package on how the organization and many volunteers were serving up Thanksgiving dinner for anyone in need. With all the government buildings closed for the holiday, it was clear we would be heading to the Salvation Army for a package on Thanksgiving dinner for those in need.

Fred started shooting video while I was preparing the head of the Salvation Army for an interview. As I waited for Fred to finish up getting the footage, I noticed someone.

It was the man I picked up on that rainy summer night.

I caught his eye and waved to him. He saw me, but did not acknowledge my wave. Either he forgot meeting me a few months prior to that day or he just didn't want a reminder of what was likely a failed attempt to find a family member in Utica earlier in the summer.

It's odd that I would recall that story after so many years. I have visited a number of homeless shelters and have encountered many people panhandling or just down on their luck over the past four decades. But that first encounter with that nameless hitchhiker comes back to me just like it happened four days ago.

Chapter 5- I'm Andy, my friend. What's your name?

August 2, 1979 Sportscast- "New York Yankees catcher Thurman Munson was killed in the crash of a small aircraft he was piloting at the Akron-Canton Airport in Ohio. A seven-time all-star and three-time Golden Glove winner, Munson appeared in all three recent World Series runs from 1976 through 1978. He played for the Binghamton Triplets in 1968, hitting .301 in what would be the last season for the Triplets.

Allow me to take you back to a time when there were no cell phones, no Facebook, no Starbucks, and no email.

That's when I met Andy.

I lived in an apartment building in Johnson City, New York. I knew no one other than work colleagues. My girlfriend lived nearly an hour away. I was a recent college graduate with the good fortune to land a great job just one week after getting my diploma.

But it was a new place and I didn't know anyone.

My broadcasting professor from Herkimer College sent me a note congratulating me on my new job. In the note, he offered some advice on how to find success as a broadcaster in a new city. Professor Dave Champoux's advice was to get to know the community as quickly as possible.

I took his advice seriously. For eight hours a day, I met the government officials who we interviewed for most of the stories that aired on the station newscasts. After work, I walked around town trying to get the lay of the land and meet the people who made up my audience.

That's when I met Andy.

He was an elderly man who I would see crossing the street at a moderately busy intersection between my apartment and where he lived.

He did not use a cane or a walker. He just slowly and steadily made his way across the street.

At first, I greeted him with a smile. I saw him taking a walk just about every day. Later encounters would be met with a wave and a small bit of conversation.

Soon, it seemed like I kept running into him practically every day. He always had something to say.

"Nice weather we've been having?"

"The roads are busy today."

"Boy, there sure is a lot of traffic."

It wasn't long before he took an important first step and introduced himself.

"I'm Andy, my friend. What's your name?"

I introduced myself and started a friendship that would last the entire time I worked in the Southern Tier region of New York State. Soon, I would not just pass by on my daily walks. I'd take a few moments to walk with him. After all, I reasoned, someone should be with him as he tried to cross the busy street.

Within weeks, he opened a door to a stronger friendship with a simple question.

"Want to play checkers?"

That question caught me by surprise. *Do I want to play checkers?* I ran his question back through my head. Without giving it much thought, I said yes.

That began a weekly visit to where Andy lived with his daughter and son-in-law at their home just a few blocks from where I lived. Every Thursday night, Andy would greet me at the door and point me to a card table with two chairs.

On that table was a checkerboard with the pieces ready for the first game. Every week, we'd play for a couple of hours, and then shake hands at the end of the last game before leaving. I think his daughter was relieved that her dad wasn't out for a walk as darkness set in.

To paraphrase an often used line about competition, our weekly games were really not about the checkers. Our visits were about bonding as friends.

He told me about how much he regarded the writings of Norman Vincent Peale who expounded the power of positive thinking. I'd share a story about a news interview I had done that week.

He would tell the story about the founders of the Endicott-Johnson Shoe Company. I told him how I found a special on Genesee Beer for 99-cents a six pack.

"Did you know that Mr. Johnson saw to it that every child in the Triple Cities got a new pair of shoes at the beginning of the school year?" he asked me one week.

"Did you know that I saw Dr. Norman Vincent Peale speak back in the 1950s?" he asked me another week.

"So, how is that young lady you're seeing?" he inquired. "When am I going to meet her?"

Every week, Andy would bring up something from his past experiences. He could keep the discussion moving along, all the time keeping his eyes on the game in front of him.

We had pleasant conversations over the checkerboard.

After a few weeks of playing checkers, Andy asked me if I wanted to learn the game of chess.

For about a month, he'd walk me through the basic moves, share some strategy, and consistently beat me game after game.

He never relented in his competitiveness while at the same time helping me to understand how the successful player gets to that place. His simple advice: "Always be thinking of the next move, the move after that, and the move after that one."

I'll never forget the night I finally beat him fair and square. As he offered his hand in congratulations, I never saw a bigger smile from a more proud teacher. After that night, we generally split the number of games won, with a slight edge going to him.

Eventually, Andy would meet Vaune. The two were immediate friends. His natural curiousity meshed well with Vaune's inquisitive nature.

When Andy's daughter gave her dad a birthday party, both Vaune and I were invited to the house for dinner and cake. Andy was grateful to his daughter for keeping a roof over his head.

"That's my Mabel," he'd say as she brought snacks to us during a break in our weekly chess game. "She is an angel sent to me from the Lord above."

Mabel's husband kept busy during our games by tending to his volunteer work coordinating activities at their church. I would often hear him making calls to other volunteers to secure usher coverage for the upcoming Sunday service.

"Yes, you offer your arm to the lady...but don't force her to take it...yes, and you lead her down to whichever pew her husband wants them to sit...yes, now you got it."

When my television station decided to do a promotional campaign on the members of the news team, thirty-second commercials were produced showing each news personality doing something fun.

News director Mark was featured preparing a campfire while out in the wilderness with his recreational vehicle. My commercial featured Andy and me playing chess. As we played our game, the announcer spoke, "When he's not working on a story for the newscast, Steve is spending time with his friends and neighbors."

Andy was among my first neighbors when I lived in Johnson City.

Ours was a friendship that was lasting and memorable.

Chapter 6- A Ring Under the Beer Can

October 2, 1979 Newscast- "Pope John Paul the second celebrated a Catholic Mass tonight in New York's Yankee Stadium. The Pope told the packed-in crowd estimated at over seventy-thousand to remain faithful to the Church and the teachings of the Catholic faith."

As summer rolled into autumn, I was moving into a new time in my young adult life.

Now that I had a couple of new suits, and a new vehicle, I had to start saving money for a very important purchase.

Vaune and I had been dating since 1976. There was no doubt we'd get married someday. Now that we were both working, separated by about forty miles on highway seventeen, we were getting more serious about a wedding date.

We looked around in Binghamton area jewelry stores to get ideas on the kind of engagement ring she might like.

I started saving as much as I could from my WICZ paychecks so that I could get her the best ring I could afford. She had a credit card but I did not have one. I was not going to borrow using her credit card. This had to be a purchase I would make.

By the fall of 1979, I felt as though I had enough saved up to make the purchase. I went to one of the stores we looked into when both of us were shopping around. I found what I felt was just the right ring.

The ring sat in its velvet box. I hid it underneath a beer can with the bottom removed in my collection of beer cans hanging on my living room wall. The collection started in college. One suggestion to anyone considering beer can collecting: think long and hard about packing up those cans every time you move. I stopped collecting a few years later and now keep about twenty vintage cans as reminders of the time when I had a wall full of them.

With the ring safely out of sight underneath a beer can, I was now looking to find the right date to propose. She knew it would be coming some time, but we both wanted the element of surprise. We wanted to do it right.

We visited my parents one weekend in October. I packed the ring and had every expectation of proposing while at a restaurant we both liked. I even showed the ring to my parents the afternoon before.

But something did not feel right. I'm not sure whether it was the service at the restaurant, the noise, or just my nerves. I couldn't do it that night.

The next Saturday night we were back in the Southern Tier. We went out to dinner, and I knew the timing was right.

She said yes.

Wedding plans started almost immediately with Vaune working with her mother, father, and sister on all the details that go into a wedding from the bride's side of the family. On the other side, I asked my brother Terry to be my best man, and asked my good friend Tim along with Vaune's brother David to be my attendants. Keep in mind it was 1979, some of the gender roles for weddings were different then. I had no problem with Vaune taking on the lion's share of the planning. If you ask her, she probably preferred it that way.

One thing that did not change was the requirement that Catholic couples attend Pre-Cana marriage conferences. Ours was held over two Sunday afternoons at a church in downtown Binghamton. The conferences included testimonials from married couples and some workshops on how to better know your partner. We both had to fill out forms individually about the things we value. This was followed by a sharing of one another's forms, some private discussion among the couples, and some group sharing.

While we'd spend our weekends going over plans for a July 1980 wedding, every Thursday night I'd head over to Andy's to play chess. I had kept him posted on my plans to propose to Vaune. After the engagement was official, I kept him updated on the wedding plans.

And every day, I went to work trying to become the best local television journalist I could be.

Chapter 7 Continuous Improvement

November 5, 1979 Newscast- "Over fifty American embassy staff employees have been taken hostage by what appears to be a group of college students in Tehran, Iran. The students stormed the embassy yesterday. The State Department is working through diplomatic channels demanding an immediate release.

Wedding preparations went on throughout early 1980 while I continued learning the local television news business. I covered some interesting stories during that last half of 1979 and the first half of 1980.

In my opinion, election night is sort of the *World Series* for television news. Taking their cues from the broadcast networks, local stations would fancy up their studio sets, bring on extra help, and try to bring viewers the results from key races faster than the competition.

Extra help generally came from the station staff being asked to assist with everything from gathering information from the Board of Elections to ordering food to be brought in for the studio based team.

We tried to spruce up our presentation for election night in 1979. Our biggest local races were for supervisors in a couple of townships in the viewing area. I was stationed at the Board of Elections office armed only with my reporter pad, pen, pager, and a pocket full of dimes to call in results to the station. Mark handled things at the station. I doubt we beat our competition at WBNG with the fastest results, but I know we did our best with the resources we had.

That first election night for me set the stage for the next fourteen years in television news. Over those years, I would report live from campaign headquarters, produce coverage for three other stations, and even called in results from the board of elections the year I left the business in 1994.

1980 was a presidential election year, so candidates and their surrogates were traveling to Binghamton to make stump speeches. I had a strong interest in national politics fueled by my weekly subscriptions to the top three national news magazines: *Time, Newsweek,* and *US News and World Report.* In 1980, those magazines were much thicker than *Time* is now. (*Newsweek and US News* stopped publishing a hard copy of their issues in 2012 and 2010 respectively, both now are available on the internet)

Coming through the Triple Cities for the 1980 presidential campaign and the New York State primary was President Jimmy Carter's son Chip. Chip was probably dispatched to the Triple Cities primarily because the area was not considered important enough to send someone with a more robust political resume. President Carter had assumed a "Rose Garden" strategy and remained in the White House to work on ending the hostage crisis. The President's surrogates were being dispatched all over the country throughout the primary season.

George H. W. Bush came to town to try to break up the momentum Ronald Reagan had created in the Republican primaries. Not many people had heard of Bush in 1980. He was campaigning as an underdog and while he did not win New York, he did win in the early primaries of Massachusetts and Connecticut. Reagan's daughter Maureen hit the campaign trail through New York and stopped by Binghamton to meet reporters.

In early 1980, former President Gerald Ford headlined a Republican fund raiser at a banquet hall near my apartment in Johnson City. The press was kept way in the back of the room.

But it was exciting to be covering this small part of *Campaign 80*.

I also interviewed Mario Cuomo on one of his stops in the region. He was Lieutenant Governor in 1980 promoting some initiative from Governor Hugh Carey's office. I don't remember why he was in town, but I remember arriving to the press availability late and dealing with a handler who basically chastised me for being late and effectively telling me that when you snooze you lose.

Observing my argument that we could set up our camera and ask a couple of questions in a matter of minutes, Cuomo came over to me, smiled, and then told his handler that he had the time to speak to my camera and me. Mario Cuomo would eventually become Governor of New York in the early 1980s.

Celebrities along the way during that short time with WICZ included George Takei from *Star Trek*, game show panelist Kitty Carlisle, and Mary Kay Ash of the *Mary Kay* make-up line.

Another famous person I met had nothing to do with a story I covered.

Throughout the year, the station would run commercials for Mount Airy Lodge in the Poconos. Every year in the off season, the Lodge would have the station employees as guests for a weekend.

Vaune and I went the September after we were married. We had a lot of fun with our coworkers enjoying the surroundings. On Saturday night, we were invited to the floor show in the Lodge's big showroom. The headliner was the "king of one-liners" Henny Youngman.

Even in 1980, Henny was not necessarily the first name you thought about as far as cutting edge comedy was concerned. But his show was entertaining and his violin playing was tolerable.

While we were waiting for his show to start, I headed to the lobby when I noticed an older gentlemen slowly making his way in my direction. As we got closer, I discovered it was Henny right there in the flesh. I said hello, and he smiled and said hello back to me. Within minutes, he got to the side of the stage and waited to be introduced. I saw no manager, no handlers, nothing that would even hint at an entourage. He was just a working comic going to the job site.

I interviewed Howard Jarvis, the man responsible for leading an effort to keep property taxes level in California. He visited Binghamton to promote a referendum and initiative effort that would make it easier for citizens to place proposed legislation on ballots. In California, Jarvis headed a group that started a drive to place *Proposition 13* on the ballot. The initiative forced local governments to end a practice of increasing property tax values practically automatically. The Howard Jarvis Taxpayers' Association lives on in California, pointing out to voters potentially expensive tax laws. Jarvis became something of a celebrity after leading the charge in California. He was featured in a cameo for the movie *Airplane* as the traveler waiting in an airport taxi throughout the entire film.

The most important story I covered during that period was the annual meeting of the Appalachian Regional Commission. The Commission was a regional collaborative of states in the Appalachian Mountain Region. New York State was one of the collaborative partners and it was the State's turn to host. Since the Triple Cities fell within the region, the City of Binghamton was selected to host the meeting.

The Appalachian Regional Commission meetings were important to me because it ran for three days. I spent each day imbedded in the conference. I immersed myself in the issues being discussed by the presenters. I filed nightly reports on the six and eleven o'clock news. Our station did not have live-from-the-field reporting capability then, but I treated the coverage of the conference with the intensity of an ever-unfolding story.

We did the most we could do with the limitations we had. Mark was tenacious about checking with local law enforcement contacts. He'd call them at least an hour before every newscast. Some of those contacts would call him to provide information on arrests or public safety matters.

We also had a lot of laughs while putting our nightly newscasts together. Rick did a lot of impressions. My favorite impression by him was Maurice Chevalier. Now that may seem a little strange given that hardly anyone knows who Chevalier was let alone what his voice was like. But I remember the French actor/singer/dancer from some films he made before his death in the early 1970s. Mark did an impression of former New York Governor Nelson Rockefeller. All three of us needed an occasional release from the high pressure environment of putting a nightly newscast on the air.

Our station manager Jesse Pevear had come to the station from Alabama. He had a distinct southern accent and came across as friendly and approachable. Jesse even did weekly editorials at the end of a newscast. It was genuine.

Jesse was a member of Binghamton Rotary Club and he would occasionally invite either Mark or me along with Peg or whoever was our photographer working that day, to join him for lunch at the Rotary meeting. I had to work for my lunch because Jesse would ask the club president to call upon the WICZ reporter to do a brief news update for the club. I enjoyed attending the meetings, but I could not go every week as my news reporting commitments required me to be out in the field. But attending Binghamton Rotary Club meetings and seeing the work they did set the stage for my joining the local Rotary clubs in three communities over the years.

My work at the station wasn't limited to reporting news. Early in my tenure, I was the lead host for a tennis tournament at a local club. I played tennis at a club level in high school and occasionally would play with friends, but that was about the extent of my qualifications as a host for a two-hour broadcast. A pro at the club served as an analyst and did most of the heavy lifting.

Fred Heckman would host a five-minute weekly hunting and fishing report during the seasons when hunters and fishermen were making their way outdoors to pursue their sports. When

Fred was on vacation, I was given the opportunity to fill his shoes. The only exposure I had to this type of reporting was watching Fred's weekly report, and seeing WKTV's Jack Fredericks do a half-hour *Outdoor Sportsmen Show* broadcast from Utica. Under Fred's direction, I made the calls to various agencies throughout the Southern Tier to check on fishing and hunting conditions, and would do my best to fill Fred's boots. Thankfully for me, no video tape from my *Outdoor Sports Report* broadcasts are known to exist. To steal a line from Johnny Carson, any film of the *Outdoor Sports Report* that I hosted has been converted to flammable nitrate stock (Carson would also add the explainer "You see, it's usually the other way around.)

Our six o'clock newscast would feature a five-minute community affairs interview called *Close-Up*. This was the place where organizations promoting events could get on the air for a few minutes. I was assigned to doing *Close-Up*. Fortunately, I rarely had to book a guest. The area non-profits came to us for the free airtime. We'd try to tape two or three segments in one block of studio time.

One time, an account representative asked me whether I'd have any interest in interviewing movie director Russ Meyer. Meyer's films were adult comedies, but even through the lens of the free-for-all seventies, he really did not belong on a local newscast. Against my better judgement, I agreed to interview Meyer. I found him to be an interesting person who brushed aside my question about whether his films might be contributing to moral decay in the nation with a simple retort, "I'm a working man doing all of this for fun and profit." Fortunately, the interview aired and there was no response, positive or negative, from it.

I also got an opportunity to be one of the hosts from the local segments of the *Jerry Lewis Labor Day Telethon*. WICZ was an affiliate of the Telethon's "Love Network". For two years, I donned the tuxedo and supported the primary host Mark as we broadcast local segments from the Oakdale Mall in Johnson City.

I hosted some of the early morning segments while Mark got some rest. It was fun doing that form of live television. The Labor Day Telethon carried so much meaning for the Muscular Dystrophy Association, the people with the disease, the caregivers, our viewers, and those of us who worked on the broadcast.

Nearly two decades later, Jerry Lewis was appearing in Rochester, New York with the Broadway show *Damn Yankees*. A coworker told me Jerry would be accepting an award from the County of Monroe at a ceremony taking place at the Hyatt Regency in downtown Rochester. By that time, I was out of the television news business. But that did not stop me from calling a friend at one of the television stations where I had worked. My friend told me to meet him at the Hyatt and walk in to the news conference with him.

Jerry accepted the award, and then took questions from the local media. He mentioned how he was writing a book on his recollections from the Martin and Lewis partnership. As none of the reporters covering the news conference picked up on that piece of information, I decided to exercise my curiosity.

I asked Jerry whether it was difficult to go back and recall that period of time. The Martin and Lewis partnership ended acrimoniously after about ten years. Jerry looked at me, smiled and said something to the effect, "Not really, it was a very special time in my life, in both our lives. I didn't want to lose those memories with time."

The book became *Dean and Me*, and was co-written by James Kaplan. Mr. Kaplan was interviewed shortly after the news broke that Jerry had passed away at his home in Las Vegas. The interviewer, pressed for time, wrapped up a five-minute live interview by asking him to describe Jerry in one word. Without giving it an extra second to think, Mr. Kaplan answered "genius".

Jerry's son Chris spoke at a meeting of Fresno Rotary I attended several years ago. Chris was raising money on behalf of the non-profit organization providing wheel chairs for people living in third world countries. While not mentioning his dad's name directly, it was clear he wanted to keep the legacy of Jerry Lewis as a champion of the handicapped moving forward.

We learned after the passing of Jerry Lewis that he was not generous toward his five sons from his first marriage. He expressly stated in his will that the sons were not to receive any portion of his estate. Unfortunately, that shades my perception of the kind of person he was. He was a humanitarian who did more to move the needle on neurological disease research than any person in history. Yet his apparent lack of compassion as expressed in his will leave me wondering why.

What I remembered fondly about the two telethons I worked on was how the local office of the Muscular Dystrophy Association expressed their gratitude to the station for producing the Binghamton portions of the broadcast. About a month after the event, we were invited to a buffet dinner in a church basement where each employee who participated in the production of the local portions of the event was given a certificate of appreciation. It was nice to be recognized by the organization.

It was a dream-come-true for me to be part of that incredible display of emotion and endurance on Labor Day.

Chapter 8-The Big Day

February 22, 1980 Sportcast- "A gold medal and an upset for the ages in US Olympic history tonight. The United States Olympic Hockey team, considered an underdog, has defeated the Soviet Union team 4 to 3 in Lake Placid."

There are a lot of things a married person remembers about his or her wedding day. I remember many details. There was the ceremony, the reception, and the honeymoon that come to mind immediately. But a special memory for me from that weekend was the rehearsal party held the Friday night before the wedding.

My dad used his membership in the Boonville Elks Club to secure the Ilion Elks lodge for the party. The local club catered a buffet held right after the rehearsal at the church. The Ilion lodge was in the same block as the church.

What made it stand out for me was the unifying of two families. Most of the bride's relatives had never met the relatives from the groom's side. The dinner, preceded by appetizers at my soon-to-be in-laws house, was a great start to what has now become a now four-decade marriage.

The rehearsal party gave me a chance to greet my college buddies who made the trip. Ray was my first roommate from my first semester at Herkimer College. At the time, he was working in his hometown of Albany. While we spoke on occasion over the previous four or five years, this was the first time I saw him in person since my sophomore year in college.

Tim is a friend I met at Syracuse. He was one of my ushers for the ceremony. Over the wedding weekend, my college friends Matt, Guf, and Rick were welcomed guests.

The rehearsal party got us all in the right mood for what was to come the next day. But for me, it really signified that two families were coming together thanks to the blessing of matrimony.

After Vaune and I said goodnight, I headed to a local motel where my family had booked some rooms for the out-of-town family members. The motel had a small bar, so after saying goodnight to everyone, my brother Terry and my friend Tim went to the bar to have a "farewell to bachelorhood" bottle of Genesee Beer. When we finished the beer, we all headed back to our rooms to go to sleep. That was the closest thing I had to a bachelor's party. But I never felt as though I missed out on anything. I was surrounded by family and good friends. I was about to get married. It was a very happy time leading up to the most important day in my life.

Vaune and I were married in July at Annunciation Catholic Church in Ilion, New York. A wedding reception was held at Twin Ponds Country Club in Utica. Matt and Guf drove members of the wedding party from the church to the reception. A friend of my sister-in-law arranged to have a limo for the maid-of-honor and best man. A friend of Vaune's arranged for a special limo for the bride and groom. We honeymooned in New York City.

There was really no question where we would spend our honeymoon. We both loved Broadway shows. About six years prior to our honeymoon, we both took part in a bus tour to the Big Apple organized by our Herkimer College music professor Joe Delorenzo.

In 1980 I had one week of vacation so we had to make the most of our time in New York City.

We took the Amtrak from the Utica train station Sunday morning. Upon arrival at Grand Central Station, we took a taxi to the Hotel Edison. That was the same hotel Joe had booked for the college trip a few years before.

When we got out of the taxi, I saw a news ticker sign that read "The former Shah of Iran, has died of cancer. Mohammad Reza Pahlavi died while in exile in Egypt. Earlier in the year, he received treatment for the disease in the US." That was the only news I saw, read, or heard about during that honeymoon week.

After dinner at Beefsteak Charlies, we took in our first show at Radio City Music Hall

The WICZ community affairs director had arranged for us to get a VIP tour of NBC at Radio City as well as tickets to a relatively new morning talk show hosted by an up and coming personality named David Letterman.

The Letterman show was the first part of our studio tour, and it was a blast. The show was only on television a few months, but you could see some of the techniques Dave and his writers were experimenting with that would appear in his late night shows that ran on NBC and later on CBS from 1982 to 2015.

Immediately following the show, Dave went into the audience to tape promotional announcements for the next five shows. He sat right in front of us for the promos. We were seen by friends and family for several days while we were away.

Tours of NBC were suspended in the late 1970s due to security concerns, so our VIP tour was extra special. We saw *NBC Nightly News* anchor John Chancelor in the hallway while our escort was taking through the various studios.

Tours resumed in the 1980s and today, the NBC Studio Tour is a popular tourist site for visitors.

Throughout the rest of the week, we saw three Broadway shows (*Children of a Lesser God, Annie*, and *Peter Pan*), toured the United Nations, walked through Central Park, and took in both the Museum of Natural History and the Museum of Broadcasting. While at the Museum of Broadcasting, a local news team was doing a story. The reporter interviewed me on what I liked about the museum. I told him I was trying to figure out what Ozzie Nelson's job was on the Ozzie and Harriet show (*The Adventures of Ozzie and Harriet*). I could not figure it out at the museum, and I believe it remains one of those unknown mysteries in television history.

Another memory that stands from that week in the Big Apple was Frank Sinatra's interpretation of the song *New York, New York*. Sinatra recorded the song earlier in the year, and it was quite popular even on some Top Forty radio stations. But on the streets of New York City, I felt as though I was hearing it all the time. Those shop owners who sold electronics such as boom boxes and cameras would blast the song from their speakers onto the streets. I heard it in the hotel lobby and in the taxi cabs. The song remains a favorite of mine. I saw Frank Sinatra perform it live on stage twice in his later years. Everytime I hear it, I return to those wonderful memories of the summer of 1980.

We took the train back to Utica on Thursday, opened our wedding gifts at Vaune's parents' home that night, and then headed to our newly rented apartment in Owego, New York Friday morning.

We assembled a scrapbook of memories from our wedding and honeymoon. After all these years, it is fun to look back on the things we saved from that miraculous week.

We have napkins from restaurants where we dined, *Playbill* programs from the Broadway shows we saw, several handwritten pages of details from what we experienced each day, a postcard from our room at the Hotel Edison, and other items. Every once in awhile, we take out that scrapbook and travel back to a week of wonder and joy over the start of a new life together as a married couple.

Children would come in a few years, jobs might change, and we could count on there always being a mix of good and challenging times. But that scrapbook sitting on a shelf represents the early stages of hope and promise. We have assembled several memory books and photograph albums from our four decades together. But the wedding and honeymoon scrapbook started it all.

By the following Monday, I was back to work. I was now doing a night shift that allowed me to anchor the eleven o'clock news.

Vaune would return to her job as a speech therapist in the Waverly Central School District later in the fall. We were a young newlywed couple and loving every moment of it.

Little did we know that a new opportunity was about to emerge.

Chapter 9- The Next Move

March 21, 1980 Sportscast- "President Carter has ordered a boycott of the Summer Olympic Games to be held this summer in the Soviet Union. The White House says the boycott is in retaliation for the Soviet invasion of Afghanistan. The games are to be held in Moscow."

In 1980, it was important to me that I think critically about where I was and where I needed to be professionally.

It was drilled into me from my admissions interview at Herkimer College right on through to my graduation four years later at Syracuse. If you wanted to move up in the broadcasting business, you had to be willing to move on.

My broadcasting professor Mr. Champoux put it more bluntly to my freshman class at Herkimer saying, "If you want to be King Kong, you've got to go to where the Empire State Building is."

The Binghamton television coverage area was considered a small market. At the time, New York City was the number one market, Los Angeles number two, and Chicago number three. Binghamton was somewhere in the one-hundred, twenties.

Deep down inside me, I knew that the day would come when it would be time to leave for a larger market. Lots of broadcasters stayed in smaller and medium markets all their professional careers. Many had positions and salaries that made even thinking about moving up not so attractive. Many had families, friends, and community networks that meant even more than bigger paychecks.

There was a part of me that felt as though maybe I could find that level of professional satisfaction if I just stayed right there in the Triple Cities. But being recently married and full of dreams of bigger and better professional challenges, my wife and I both believed that if we were really serious about moving up the ladder, sooner would be better than later.

At the same time, WICZ went through a budget cut. I was moved back to the night shift following the job cuts of two news department employees. At age twenty-three and surviving a round of budget tightening, I knew now was the time to start looking for a new job.

For a young broadcaster with eyes on moving up in market size in the late 1970s and early 1980's, *Broadcasting* magazine was where the search started. The annual subscription was about $35 back then, but it was considered the bible of television and radio and worth every penny.

The magazine would have articles about pending rulings of the Federal Communications Commission (FCC), features on up and coming as well as senior broadcast executives, news of emerging technology in the industry, and a section on recent promotions at television and radio stations.

Programming and station management read *Broadcasting* for the advertisements. Syndicators would launch their sales campaigns for network sitcoms and dramas that had assembled enough episodes (usually one-hundred episodes in the early 1980s) to be run during the local access time periods when stations could program whatever they wanted for their audiences. Talk shows and game shows were commonly advertised for stations on the pages of *Broadcasting*. Within a couple of years, the new genre of the entertainment-news program would begin with *Entertainment Tonight* and its many imitators.

Broadcast sales managers would read *Broadcasting* to learn of some product launch plans from major advertising agencies. Sometimes a tip first read in *Broadcasting* might result in a lead that could generate revenue for a station.

Broadcast engineers kept *Broadcasting* close by to determine whether new FCC rules might mean additional equipment needs for a station.

Production managers had their eye on the newest studio and live remote equipment generally previewed in the pages of the magazine.

For someone looking for the next move in the television or radio business, the articles could wait. We were most interested in those open positions found in the classified ads.

I would scour the weekly classified ads in *Broadcasting* looking for jobs. Checking the column on recent promotions would sometimes signal that a position might be opening up. For me, a person getting promoted was a good thing because that usually meant a job might be opening up to fill the spot vacated by the person who was recently moved up.

I would answer the ads, make the calls, and even took a few information interviews. Information interviews were the ones where no job was known to be open, but either the news director or the potential hire got together just to talk about the station. Those information interviews were all about getting the news director familiar with my work.

I sent out audition video tapes to several stations, got a nice collection of rejection letters, and three bona-fide interviews. I tried not to grow frustrated with the process. After all, I reasoned, I had a job in the industry. If I remained at this station I would just use the time to get more experience in my craft.

One night in late September, I got a call in the newsroom shortly after the six o'clock newscast. That call would change my career.

Chapter 10- The Offer

May 18, 1980 Newscast- "The eruption of Mount St. Helens in Washington has triggered a massive avalanche. Fifty-seven people have been killed, but officials say that number would have been much higher had citizens not heeded repeated warnings of seismic activity at the volcano site."

The news director from WAAY-TV in Huntsville, Alabama interviewed me over the phone. At the end of our half-hour conversation, he invited me to fly to Huntsville at the station's expense to see the facility, meet the station manager, and see if this opportunity to report three days a week and co-anchor the weekend newscasts was right for me.

For Vaune, the opportunity was more about taking the next step in a big adventure. For me, the chance to move up several notches in market size, coupled with a chance to work in a larger news department, made the choice simple. Either one of us could have spiked the deal. But we moved forward to the interview stage.

The day before I was to fly out to Huntsville for the interview, we saw Mark and his wife at the wedding reception of a WICZ employee. Throughout the days since the first call from the station in Huntsville, we struggled with whether or not I should tell Mark about what was going on. Vaune convinced me that seeing Mark at the wedding was, on one level, a sign that I should disclose to him what was happening.

Now was the right time. I took in a deep breath as I was about to tell the person who gave me my first full time television news reporting job that I might be leaving.

I asked Mark for a few private minutes in the hallway at the reception hall. We discussed the opportunity. I'm sure the thought crossed his mind that if I got the job in Huntsville, my position at the station would likely not be filled. The news team he had built was already being taken apart little by little due to station budget cuts. He was probably coming to the realization that it would probably be up to a new group of station leadership to take channel forty to the next level.

He thanked me for coming to him before taking the interview. He wished me well and assured me that the plane trip would go nice and easy.

My first airplane ride ever was from the Broome County Airport outside of Binghamton. I took a commuter airline to Washington, DC where I connected with a small jet heading to Huntsville.

I was picked up at the airport by the news director and immediately driven to the Hunstville Hilton. I put my bags in my room, and joined the news director for dinner in the hotel dining room.

Following dinner, the news director took me up Monte Sano Boulevard overlooking the City of Hunstville to the station. Like a lot of older local television facilities, the broadcast tower was next to the station. The news department was on the second floor of the building.

It was Sunday night, so the staff was smaller than what the station might have on a week day. I met the Assignment Editor who was pulling double duty and co-anchoring the weekend newscast. I also met the woman who would be my co-anchor.

It was clear to me that this news department was exactly what I needed for my second job in television. The station had a live truck; in fact, the term "Live Eye" was trademarked by the station in the late 1970s. The staff of about twenty was about five times the size of the size of the team I worked with in

Binghamton. They were equipped with a wire service, state-of-the-art video cameras for use in the field, and even a news bureau in the northwestern part of the viewing area.

The station programmed a seven-day a week news service and was currently locked in a battle for the top spot with the local CBS affiliate. It had healthy competition, a commitment to news, and the modern tools of electronic news gathering.

The news director and I stayed for the first half of the ten o'clock news (being in the Central Time Zone meant the late news started an hour earlier than in the Eastern Zone). We then headed back down Monte Sano Boulevard. He dropped me off at the hotel and told me we'd talk to the station manager the next morning.

On Monday morning, I met the station manager. He asked me about my long term goals. I recall answering that I wanted to have a successful career as a television journalist. After a few additional inquiries about my work experience, I was invited to ask questions. I asked why there were so many openings in the news department. The news director explained that people simply moved on up their career paths, thereby creating openings within the ranks.

The interview went well. I spent a couple of hours in the newsroom before being taken back to the airport in the early afternoon. By mid-afternoon, I boarded a plane and was back in Binghamton later that evening. On Tuesday, I was back on the job at WICZ. Now was the time for waiting and wondering whether I might be leaving.

Apparently the station manager signed off on the news director's recommendation that I get the job. By the end of the week I was offered the position. Vaune and I mulled it over and decided that at this early stage of our marriage, this might be a good idea.

The following Monday, I told Mark I would be leaving in two weeks. He wished me well and hinted that he might be leaving in the coming months. That disclosure made me feel even better about the decision to leave the station in Binghamton. I knew I would miss my co-workers, my viewers, and the relative close proximity to family living in upstate New York.

Telling our families was tough. Both sides likely assumed Vaune and I would remain in New York State throughout our married lives. Both families realized that opportunities would cross our paths and they understood our decision.

Now I had to break the news to the staff at channel forty.

Chapter 11- Moving On

June 1, 1980 Newscast- "Atlanta businessman Ted Turner has launched the nation's only 24-hour news network. The Cable News Network, or C-N-N went on the air at 6 o'clock this evening from its headquarters in Atlanta."

There would be a few regrets about my time at the Binghamton television station. Looking back, it amazes me that I did such a variety of things. News, sports, tennis matches, telethons, interview programs, even an outdoorsman segment.

Given my interest in game shows, I would later regret that there was no opportunity to do something in that space. Some local stations were producing high school quiz programs during that time. Maybe it would have eventually happened at channel forty. It would have been fun to develop and host a local high school quiz program.

I also wished I had embraced sports broadcasting more. While I never wanted to be a sportscaster, I was never pleased with my work in that portion of my tenure. To do it over again, I would have worked harder to better understand what success as a sports reporter looked like.

Along those lines, if there was an opportunity to do more with weather reporting, I would have jumped at the chance. At channel forty, our weather forecast was done from the news desk with a voice-over a black and white satellite video of the United States, followed by a forecast superimposed over a nondescript background. It would have been great to have a map board and the capability to do a more extensive weather report. But with our small staff, sustaining that kind of presentation night after night might have been difficult to pull off.

There's a tinge of regret that I did not explore trying to remain connected to radio broadcasting in some way. As many television broadcasters would moonlight back in those days, it might have made sense for me to work part time at one of Binghamton's radio stations. Frankly, the thought never seriously crossed my mind at the time. My weekends were too valuable to me back then. As I said, it's only a tinge of regret.

I spent the rest of that two-week notice period saying goodbye to coworkers. They were not my first work family, but they were certainly a special group of people who took me under their wing.

Rick Krolak had left the station just a few months after I started working with him. I had stopped in at WNEP-TV in Wilkes Barre to say hello a couple of months before I got the Huntsville offer. We spoke over the phone during my two-week notice period.

Station Manager Jesse Pevear knew of the owners who would be my new bosses in Huntsville. In his genuine southern accent, he assured me they were a "quality bunch of people, and they will take good care of you".

I was also congratulated by chief engineer Gino (Rick) Riccadelli, production manager Joanne, and senior director Vern.

Rick Riccadelli was a regular technical genius when it came to finding cost effective ways to keep station equipment operating. He also knew what the limitations of a UHF station were in the early 1980s. His thoughtful analysis of the potential of our station helped me realize what I needed to do to move along in my career.

Joanne found herself thrown into the production manager role shortly before I arrived at the station, and she handled the multi-tasking that was required to survive in that environment.

She coordinated all the production for the station such as commercials, promotional announcements, and the Labor Day Telethon.

Vern was my first "coffee buddy". We started a tradition when I arrived at the station in the mid-afternoon for my night shift. He'd offer to buy me a cup of coffee if I would "fly" down to the coffee shop to pick it up. Many days I was greeted in the newsroom with Vern announcing, "If you fly, I'll buy."

One night, Vern was filling in as director of the newscast. After the six o'clock news, he suggested we go to a nicer, more expensive restaurant for dinner. I tried to keep my meals in a more affordable range, but this was going to be a one-time thing as Vern would be rotating back to his regular day shift in another week. When the check arrived, Vern grabbed it and refused to let me pay my share.

Fred Heckman was back doing morning news anchoring in the wake of station staff cuts. He was then doing the morning news cut-ins during the *Today Show*, and then would work in the production department after the news breaks were finished. He was a dear man who was devoted to his wife and mother. I told him how much I appreciated his sense of humor. He told me how much he enjoyed having me be an audience for his wit.

Others in the station wished me well. Our new director Ted was a Syracuse University grad just like me. He was working on his Masters during my senior year at SU. He replaced Jan, a technician who had replaced Rick Krolak as director/videographer for a few months before following Rick to WNEP in Wilkes-Barre. Ted helped both Vaune and me when we purchased a couch from a Binghamton furniture store that was going out of business. We got a great deal if we could deliver the couch. I called Ted, and he graciously came to our aid. Ted and I were good professional acquaintances, but I was not with the station long enough to build a stronger bond.

There was an operator in the station's master control room who extended his best wishes. While his name just doesn't register some forty years after working with him, both Vaune and I were grateful to he and his wife for inviting us to their home for an evening to watch the film classic *Citizen Kane*. I had seen the movie in a film class in college. To see it with friends in a social setting was great.

Jesse's secretary, whose name still escapes me, extended her congratulations. I never forgot how she cornered me during the United Way campaign reminding me that I was the only one on the staff who had not pledged. She urged me to make the minimum contribution "so that the station would have one-hundred percent participation." I had no idea whether she was using that same technique with other employees, but it worked in my case.

Soon it came down to the last day.

I had a teary farewell with my photographer Peg. In the early months of my tenure at the station, we worked identical hours. We saw each other over eight hours a day. Toward the end when I was moved to evenings, I'd be coming in as she was ending her shift. On that last day, she came over to me, said a quick goodbye, and ran into the break room. I followed and found her wiping away tears. Then I got a little teary-eyed.

Peg and I had been through a lot in the past year-and-a-half. We produced dozens of our so-called "quality pieces". Those quality pieces helped get me the job in Huntsville.

Mark would anchor the six o'clock news that night. I was to anchor the eleven o'clock newscast. He greeted me in the newsroom and again offered congratulations. He thanked me for my service. I thanked him for hiring me, his professionalism, and for teaching me as much as he could in a relatively short period of time.

On that last night when I was assembling the content for the eleven o'clock news, I deliberately left about thirty seconds at the very end of the broadcast so that I could say goodbye to my viewers. I don't remember the exact last words, but I probably said something like this:

> "Stay with channel forty and NBC throughout the weekend for news, and the Eyewitness News team will be back here on Monday. As for me, I'll be heading

south for a new opportunity. I thank you for watching, and I thank the group of professionals I have worked with here at channel forty. Thank you, and good night."

As hard as that last night on the air in the Triple Cities was, it did not take the emotional toll of saying goodbye to my chess partner, and first friend, Andy.

Chapter 12- Farewell My Friend

August 14, 1980 Newscast- "Workers in Gdansk, Poland, have seized the Lenin Shipyard. They are protesting rising food prices. Their leader Lech Walesa says the strike will go on for as long as it takes to get the government to lower food costs."

Missing my weekly chess games with Andy would be a change in routine for both of us. But our time as friends was all about changing our routines.

Shortly before I got married, I was moved to a night shift at work. My weekly chess matches with Andy were now played in the afternoon before my shift started. We usually split our matches about fifty-fifty. The conversation was still interesting, especially since I now could tell him how my wife was doing.

About two months before I turned in my notice at the station, Andy's daughter made the difficult decision to move him to a nursing home. I made my weekly visits to his new address at a modern assisted living facility. He'd have the game board set up in his room every Thursday afternoon.

While the changes in location and in the time of our weekly visits were necessary, I really missed the way things were when Andy and I started our weekly routine. When he lived a few blocks from my apartment, I would walk to and from his house every Thursday night. We played our matches in the living room of his daughter's home. I could hear Andy's son-in-law lining up helpers for a church project. His daughter would serve us a snack of cookies and juice about midway through our matches. Off in the distance, I could hear a television set tuned to channel forty where a new NBC series *Buck Rogers in the 25th Century* was on every Thursday night from 8:00 to 9:00. I never saw the show, but I know I heard most of the episodes from the first season.

But life is about change, and both Andy and I were adaptable. After all, I was open to change when he proposed that we switch from checkers to chess.

But this change would be permanent. Deep down, we knew that we would not pass this way again.

I told him about the job offer right after I gave my two weeks-notice. He was a little surprised that I would be leaving, but knew that I was pursuing a career in television news and that I needed to move on. I'm sure his daughter helped him understand why I needed to leave the Triple Cities.

On that last afternoon we played chess, we both knew a special time was coming to an end.

We parted with a handshake, and this time, a hug.

He told me he thought of me like I was his son. I thanked him for taking that important first step of introducing himself to me.

I left with tears in my eyes and gratitude for having this important first friend as I started my professional life. As I left his room that afternoon, I knew that I would probably never see him again.

I thought about that first day when he introduced himself to me on a busy street crossing in Johnson City. I thought about how he eventually invited me to play checkers with him every Thursday night at his daughter's home and how the weekly game changed from checkers to chess. I remembered the first chess game I won, and how proud he was that his student beat the teacher. I thought about how we moved the time of the weekly game to accommodate his move to the skilled nursing facility and adjusted as I took on a night shift at work.

But most of all, I thought about our friendship. A bond that covered four generations, a lot of local history from the Triple Cities, and a trust that we were good friends now and forever.

We were planning our next move, and the move after that, and the move after that one.

Chapter 13- Leaving Town

October 2, 1980 Sportscast- "The Muhammad Ali/Larry Holmes fight was nothing either boxer should be proud of tonight in Las Vegas. The fight was stopped in the eleventh round after a clearly out of shape Ali stumbled his way through most of the bout. Holmes is the winner. Many are calling on Ali to retire from the ring. Ali blamed his poor performance on thyroid medication."

Vaune and I rented a U-Haul trailer for my move to the south. I recall having to have a trailer hitch and a lighting kit installed on the truck in order to make it all work. The new job would pay a lot more, but the new station was only going to give me a lump sum payment that covered a portion of my out-of-pocket moving costs.

We spent the weekend configuring how our furniture would fit in the limited space we had in the truck and trailer. We did most of the loading on Saturday during the day, and then finished up with covering the items in the truck bed with a heavy tarp in case I encountered rain on the trip.

Vaune would not accompany me on the trip to Huntsville. She made arrangements with a friend who had extra room. Our plan was for her to stay back in the Southern Tier to finish out the year with the school district where she worked as a speech therapist. We would be apart for about seven weeks. Now let me tell you for a couple only married just three months, seven weeks would be a long, long time.

I got an early start on the road Sunday morning with my Toyota pick-up truck box filled up, towing a U-Haul trailer packed with stuff. At that time, we lived in Owego, about twenty miles west of the Triple Cities.

Vaune and I said goodbye, and I climbed behind the steering wheel. With luck, I would be in Huntsville at the end of the next day.

It would be about nine-hundred miles from Owego, New York where we lived and Huntsville, Alabama. My plan was to knock off at least half the distance on the first night.

These were the pre-Mapquest days, so I got by with a road map of the southern United States, a cup of coffee, and some snacks. By seven o'clock, I was making my way to Huntsville.

The first trip milestone would be the Triple Cities. As I drove through the highway seventeen and Interstate eighty-one interchange in Binghamton, I tried not to let my emotions get too heavy. My truck and U-Haul were passing through the city that I called home for a year-and-a-half. Cruising at a safe sixty miles-per-hour, the truck bed tarp was holding on nicely and the U-Haul seemed to be making the trip without any problems.

Now it was time for some introspection.

The past eighteen months were my freshman year of the rest of my life. I put my education to work and took part in the best on-the-job training program a man could ask for. I earned a weekly paycheck and started paying bills including my student loan payment of about ninety-dollars every three months.

The Southern Tier was a place that introduced me to spedies and *Pat Mitchell's* ice cream. It was where I purchased my first brand new vehicle. It was where I bought the engagement ring. It was where I proposed to my girlfriend.

In that seventeen-month period, I got married.

It was where I met my first friend outside of school or college. It was where I embraced the game of chess. It was where I learned the heartache of disconnecting with a special friend and all those work colleagues.

At sixty-miles an hour, I passed through all the Binghamton highway exits off Interstate eighty-one. I looked into my rearview mirrors on the doors of my pick-up truck. The load was safe and secure.

The Triple Cities were fading away in the mirror, but never from my heart.

Chapter 14- Settled In

It was election night 1980, and I was covering the Republican victory celebration at the Huntsville Hilton in Huntsville, Alabama.

On the job less than two weeks as weekend co-anchor and news reporter for WAAY-TV, I was assigned to cover the "victory" celebration from the local banquet room at the Hilton.

Both the GOP and the Democrats called their election night parties "victory" celebrations or "watch parties". Both groups knew they would win some and lose some. The victory party was more about thanking campaign volunteers, pledging to work with the other side, and looking ahead to the next election.

Shortly after the polls close, it's clear the Reagan landslide is overwhelming the nation as well as the local viewing area in northern Alabama. Suddenly, I'm propelled to the top spot on our ten o'clock newscast. The stations "Live Eye" microwave van is being moved to where I'm stationed.

At ten o'clock, I will do my first ever live shot; reporting from the scene, interviewing the local party chairman, and answering questions from the station's studio based anchor team.

What an incredible string of events.

Just two weeks ago, I was saying farewell to colleagues and my friend Andy. Now I'm in the thick of things on the most important day in local television. What a thrill.

I wish my wife could be here to see this start to the next chapter of my professional life. But in just a few weeks, she will be here by my side.

I also wish Andy could see me now. My chess teacher would be happy for me. I'm sure he's praying for me. Regardless, he's in my corner.

He would often emphasize faith, positive thinking, and the importance of planning for the next move.

And now, moments before I file my first ever live-from-the-scene report, the director is setting up to take my camera live on the air.

Stand by live-eye, take live-eye.

Epilogue

In the early years following my departure from channel forty, I stayed in touch with only a handful of the friends and colleagues from those days in Binghamton. With the exception of Mark Williams, I lost touch with everyone.

Mark left WICZ about a year after I departed. He had posts at stations in Nebraska, Georgia, and Florida. For a few years, he was filing reports and providing analysis of news events for one of Nancy Grace's programs on cable news. Mark and I reconnected a few years ago via Facebook and we continue to keep each other posted on our lives. He recently announced his retirement from broadcasting.

Rick Krolak, my first news photographer/editor at WICZ-TV, was killed in a news helicopter crash in Phoenix, Arizona in July 2007. After WICZ, Rick had a distinguished career at WNEP in Wilkes-Barre, Pennsylvania and had moved on to KNXV in Phoenix. Rick left a family that loved him, friends who enjoyed his company, and a passion for telling stories with his video camera.

I smile when I think about the station manager's secretary cornering me to make a donation to the 1979 United Way campaign. In later years, I would volunteer for two United Way organizations as a member of the board of directors, and in 2001 as a campaign chairman. My most memorable experience from serving United Way came during the year I was chairman. With two weeks to go before the end of the campaign, the Executive Director alerted me that we were in danger of not meeting the goal. The competitive spirit, forged from my fifteen years in television news, kicked in. I cancelled my commitment to an important leadership development program event, convened an emergency meeting of our campaign team, and extracted promises from everyone to do everything they could to take us to the finish line. We met the goal.

In personal matters, my wife Vaune and I will celebrate thirty-nine years of marriage in 2019. In addition to upstate New York, our adventure together has taken us to the South, the Mid-west, and now in California where we have lived for the past fifteen years. We have two daughters, and one grandson.

In case you're wondering how those news headlines I used at the beginning of each chapter worked out, here's the update:

Dan White served five years for the manslaughter of San Francisco Mayor George Moscone and Council Member Harvey Milk. Moscone is memorialized with the naming of a convention center in San Francisco. Milk is remembered primarily as the subject of the Sean Penn movie *Milk*.

NASA's Skylab debris eventually fell in the ocean near India in July of 1979. It didn't hit anybody, other than striking the wallets of anyone who bought a "Skylab Target" t-shirt. I was assigned the NASA beat as a reporter at my next station WAAY-TV in Hunstville where I worked from 1980-1982. This assignment put me in position to cover the first three Space Shuttle launches. Thanks to a column I wrote more than three decades later following a California visit from one of the astronauts on the very last Space Shuttle mission, I think I hold a special distinction. I may be one of a handful of reporters to have interviewed members of the both the first and last Shuttle crews.

Ted Kennedy tried to give President Jimmy Carter a run for the Democratic Presidential Nomination in 1980. But the Senator's bid fell short and left a divided party to run against Republican Ronald Reagan. Reagan defeated Carter in a landslide. The first live-from-the-field report I did at WAAY-TV in Huntsville was from a hotel that served as GOP victory headquarters on the election night, 1980.

The Shah of Iran received cancer treatments, and then was flown to Panama to recover. He died on July 27, 1980, the day after my wedding. The American Hostages were held in Iran for four-hundred, forty-four days. They were released during the inauguration of Ronald Reagan on January 20, 1981.

Mount St. Helens endured subsequent eruptions after the deadly one in May 1980. It now sits stately as a curious visitor venue in the northwest United States.

CNN was sold by Ted Turner to Time Warner in 1986. It remains on the air and on line, along with other 24-hour news channels such as MSNBC, Headline News, and Fox News. I heard Ted Turner speak at a convention of the Radio Television News Directors Association in September 1982 when I was serving as news director for WTVO in Rockford, Illinois. He was proud of his two-year old news channel then and expressed his surprise that the three major networks had not launched their own 24-hour news channels before he did.

Lech Walesa became president of Poland in the wake of strong popularity following the abolition of communism in that country. He served as president from 1990-1995. Pope John Paul II, the only Polish pope, died in 2005, and was canonized a few years later. He is Saint John Paul.

In the sports headlines I used, the Montreal Canadiens ended up winning game five of the Stanley Cup Play Offs on the night of my debut on channel forty: May 21, 1979. President Carter's Summer Olympic ban held up. Muhammad Ali stayed in professional boxing for another fight. He lost his last bout against Trever Berbick in 1981, losing in a ten-round decision.

While I have no memory of any extraordinary local story from that period of time, one of the places where I gathered the news became a news story in the years after I left. In February 1981, the State of New York closed the Binghamton State Office Building after discovering PCB contamination following a transformer fire. The building was shut down for several years. Within a week of the building being closed, then Governor Hugh Carey assured reporters the building would reopen soon with his now famous comment that he would "Swallow an entire glass of PCB's and run a mile afterwards." The building reopened thirteen years later.

I have many memories from some of the national stories that occured from May 1979 to October 1980.

To this day, I remember the milestones from the Reagan/Carter presidential campaign. It was my first national election cycle as a reporter.

When I saw the tearing down of the Berlin Wall in 1989 followed by the end of the Soviet Union from 1990 to 1991, I remembered how that chain of events started with the hard fought battle by the striking workers in Poland protesting higher food prices. Pope John Paul II played a key role by keeping the plight of his homeland on the forefront of political discussion with world leaders.

When I see a natural disaster play out on a 24-hour news channel, I remember all the build up to the expected eruption of Mount St. Helens and how we covered it in 1980 using our network's video feed and information we gleaned off weather radio.

It was a pioneer time for an electronic television journalist. I was a proud and grateful participant.

Andy was in his late eighties when I left him following our last weekly chess match in October 1980. In December, from my apartment in Huntsville, Alabama, I wrote him a letter and a Christmas card.

I wasn't really surprised that I did not get a response.

Several years later, I visited Binghamton and dropped by Andy's daughter's home. She wasn't in, but her husband told me how Andy had passed away peacefully in his sleep a couple of years after I left the community.

Andy's daughter sent me a letter shortly after that visit to fill in some of the details, and to thank me for being his friend. She told me how he often spoke of our weekly chess games and that he truly cherished the time we'd spent talking to one another while carefully watching our game board.

He was much older and saw life as another chapter of his story, but not the final chapter.

In 1979, I was relatively young and just beginning to figuratively write my life story. Our paths crossed, and it changed my life.

Bonus- Selected Columns & Book Excerpt

Over the past dozen years, in addition to my books and regular columns, I've written several op/ed essays that have appeared in many newspapers across the country. What follows are five essays inspired by my experiences from working in Binghamton, New York from May 1979 to October 1980.

May 17, 2007

Kitty Carlisle Hart had the right idea about the arts. (from the Binghamton Sun Bulletin)

The passing of Kitty Carlisle Hart on Aril 18 in New York City brought back a memory from nearly three decades ago that took place in Binghamton.

I was a TV reporter at WICZ-TV, channel 40 from May 1979 to October 1980. In the fall of 1979, the regional meeting of the Appalachian Regional Commission was taking place at the then Holiday Inn in downtown Binghamton.

News Director Mark Williams instructed me to spend all my time covering this event. So for two days, I developed stories centered on the activities and initiatives of the Commission.

We did stories on poverty, water, transportation, and whatever else was on the agenda for the meeting. I enjoyed the break from running after spot news and being able to do some in-depth reporting.

Ms. Carlisle Hart attended a portion for the meeting dealing with the arts. As chair of the New York State Council on the Arts, she had already made a name for herself in advocating on behalf of the arts throughout the region.

I found her quite approachable and willing to discuss the commission and her traveling to the Triple Cities to speak out on the need for the arts to remain fully funded throughout the region.

One question I recall asking centered on how some might argue that in a time of tight budgets, cutting funding for the arts might be seen as a reasonable way to order our priorities. I remember she thanked me for raising the question, and then went on to explain why the arts should not be subjected to budget slashing.

"Arts add to the community, she stressed in her response. "The arts bring so much to a community in terms of culture and economic impact."

We used most of that interview on that nights' newscast. To this day, I think about her comments whenever an arts or cultural program is threatened financially.

She was a passionate advocate.
.

August 2007

Remembering Rick Krolak (From the Binghamton Sun Bulletin)

The midair collision of two television news helicopters last week in Phoenix became personal for me when I learned one of the four killed was someone I worked with nearly thirty years ago.

Photographer Rick Krolak was one of the four killed while covering a police chase in the city. I worked with Rick when I was a reporter for WICZ-TV in Binghamton back in 1979. Rich was a photographer there who shot and edited my first stories as a TV reporter back in the early days of electronic news gathering.

Our station was among the first in the nation to covert from film to video for news gathering. Our system included a bulky video camera and a broadcast VCR mounted on a hand truck. It was hardly portable, but the station knew video was the way to go for cost effective pictures of breaking news. Rick helped me understand the equipment limitations, and helped me understand the endless possibilities as a reporter using video as a tool to communicate.

I remember a pre-Memorial holiday weekend piece about how gas prices might impact vacationers. A gas price story has almost become a cliché in today's news circles, but in 1979 with fuel prices nearing an unheard of 90-cents a gallon, it was real news.

Another time I recall was a heavy rain and wind storm that hit the Binghamton area in the late afternoon. We both knew the potential of the pictures; so I jumped behind the wheel of our station news car and Rick sat in the passenger seat shooting video of the heavy rain and extensive damage.

Through washed out underpasses and intense winds, we got the pictures. We got back to the station in time to edit the story that night's newscast.

Rick left the station for the greener pastures of WNEP, Channel sixteen, in Wilkes-Barre, Pennsylvania that fall. We missed him right away, but knew he was happy at a station with state of the art video equipment, live trucks, and a helicopter. Rick wanted the tools to do his job in the best way possible. Channel sixteen provided him with those tools.

I spoke to him twice after he left the Southern Tier: then, as what happens with time and new opportunities, we lost contact. He left WNEP a few years later and his career eventually took him to the ABC affiliate in Phoenix.

I'll leave the debate over whether news helicopters should be patrolling overhead on news stores to those with vested interests in our right to know versus public. News coverage judgments must be made with concern over the safety of those covering the news as well as the people making the news.

I was saddened when I learned of the accident. It's hard to come to terms with knowing someone who really enjoyed his work and loved his family died doing the job he was destined to have.

But we will.

Rick would expect us to.

May 2011

You Never Forget Your First Job (From Our Community Story, MercedCountyEvents.com)

The webmaster of this site, Brad Haven, is always challenging me to provide a picture with my columns. He has explained to me how a picture can help illuminate a point. He has even sent me an article about how a picture is worth more than a thousand words.

He's right. Pictures definitely help when you're trying to tell a story.

I believe I have found another reason to look for a photograph to accompany each of my columns. So taking Brad's advice from early in this assignment, I went back to my photographs.

After the most recent post on my eight years as an altar boy, I struggled with what the next subject should be. I really don't have anything to say about the US getting Bin Laden; I'm satisfied that justice was delivered.

I could weigh in on Mother's Day, but by the time this is posted, the holiday will have passed. Maybe next year. That left me searching for the next idea.

When you encounter writer's block, go to the pictures. And that's what leads me to this photograph I found in my career scrapbook the other day.

The photo (shown in the Photos section of this book) shows a very young Steve Newvine (on the right) trying to write a television news story from the newsroom at WICZ-TV in Binghamton, New York. The year was 1979. The man on the left was my first television news boss Mark Williams. Mark had been elevated to News Director only a couple of months prior to the time this photograph was taken. I was his first hire.

Fresh out of college (Syracuse University) I interviewed for the job during my finals. I remember not being so sure I impressed him in the interview, but I had an audition tape (a video tape of stories I produced while at a college internship at another TV station).

Mark saw enough potential there is put me on his short list. He promised to get back to me by the end of the week.

He called me again on a Thursday night and said he had to run a few things past his general manager. He said he would call me Friday. I hung up the phone, announced to my parents that I wouldn't be going to sleep that night as I worried about whether I would actually be offered the job.

I did fall asleep later that night (probably early in the morning of that Friday). I stayed close to the phone all day Friday. At six-thirty PM, someone in my family suggested I go outside for a walk. I resigned myself to thinking that maybe Mark got caught up in his work of the week. I put on my sneakers and headed out the door.

Then the phone rang. It was Mark. He offered me the job. I accepted. He asked when I could start, and I said "Monday!" We wished each other a good weekend. I hung up the phone, hugged my family, and started packing for Binghamton.

I said my goodbyes to my grandparents, withdrew my life savings up to that point (about $500), and left for my first paying job in television news that weekend.

As the picture shows, I reported and wrote news for the station. Mark and I, along with four or five other staff people, made up the news department. We had no state or national wire service.

Mark had a lot of contacts throughout the viewing area that he routinely called to get tips on potential local news stories. I learned from him and the others how to produce a news story, how to assemble an entire newscast, how to shoot video when my photographer couldn't accompany me on a story, and how to connect with the local community.

During my year and a half at WICZ-TV, I did every on-air job the station had including news, weather, sports, talk show host, and outdoors sports reporter.

Station finances in 1980 forced a layoff that spared my job, but sent a chilling message to everyone that we better cover our bets and prepare for even tougher times.

I started looking for a new job shortly after returning from my honeymoon in July. In October, I left the station for WAAY-TV in Hunstville, Alabama. I stayed in television news for another fourteen years.

I'm glad I found that old picture from thirty-two years ago in my scrapbook. I exchange an occasional email from the man who hired me.

Some of the radio and television broadcasters in the Binghamton market have formed a reunion club. (Note, the reunion club is dormat as of the publication of this book.). They host a dinner and awards event every year. One of these days, I'm going to attend.

You never forget your first job. I had lots of jobs throughout high school and college that helped pay college costs and other expenses, but the first job the field that I trained in will always remain a special memory.

And I have a picture to remind me of just how special that time was.

September 2017

Labor Day Memories with Jerry Lewis (From Our Community Story, MercedCountyEvents.com)

Labor Day and Jerry Lewis. For most of my life that weekend and that person were practically one-in-the-same.

I remember watching the annual Muscular Dystrophy Telethon in my family living room. Jerry Lewis was very funny, but would frequently turn serious as he reminded everyone why it was important to call in a pledge.

His appearances on television outside of Labor Day weekend were confined mainly to talk shows, where the likes of Mike Douglas, Merv Griffin, and Johnny Carson would have him on frequently promoting a movie or an upcoming appearance in Las Vegas.

There's a show business legend that recalls one night in the early 1970s when all three late night talk shows (Carson, Griffin, and Dick Cavett) taped their shows in New York City. Jerry appeared on all three shows on the same night. He made an appearance as a regular guest on one, and then did quick cameos on the other two.

The movies had their moments. In my opinion, the films with Dean Martin were funny. None of Jerry's performances as a solo movie actor stood out for me. I enjoyed the *Disorderly Orderly* where he runs amuck in a hospital setting.

As a teen watching the annual telethon growing up in the 1970s, I hoped that one day I would have a chance to be part of that tradition.

I got my chance as one of the hosts from the Binghamton, New York affiliate of the Telethon's "Love Network". For two years, I donned the tuxedo and supported the primary host Mark Williams as we broadcast local segments from the Oakdale Mall in Johnson City. I hosted some of the early morning segments while Mark got some rest.

It was fun doing that form of live television. I left the station after two years, and even though my career would take me onward to four other television stations, none of them carried the *Labor Day Telethon*.

It was a dream-come-true for me to be part of that incredible display of emotion and endurance on Labor Day.

Nearly two decades later, Jerry Lewis was appearing in Rochester, New York with the Broadway show Damn Yankees. A coworker told me Jerry would be accepting an award from the County of Monroe at a ceremony taking place at the Hyatt Regency in downtown Rochester.

I called a friend at one of the television stations where I had worked several years earlier and asked if I could accompany him to the ceremony.

Jerry accepted the award, and then took questions from the local media. He mentioned how he was writing a book on his recollections from the Martin and Lewis partnership. I asked him whether it was difficult to go back and recall that period of time. He looked at me, smiled and said something to the effect, "Not really, it was a very special time in my life, in both our lives. I didn't want to lose those memories with time."

The book became *Dean and Me*, and was co-written by James Kaplan. Mr. Kaplan was interviewed shortly after the news broke that Jerry had passed away at his home in Las Vegas. The interviewer, pressed for time, wrapped up a five-minute live interview by asking him to describe Jerry in one word. Without giving it an extra second to think, Mr. Kaplan answered "genius".

Jerry's son Chris spoke at a meeting of Fresno Rotary I attended several years ago. Chris was raising money on behalf of the non-profit organization providing wheel chairs for people living in third world countries. While not mentioning his dad's name directly, it was clear he wanted to keep the legacy of Jerry Lewis as a champion of the handicapped moving forward.

There's no desire within me to explore the complications of Jerry Lewis. He was a gifted entertainer who used his life to help others. It was a life with purpose. Fortunately for many of us who remember those twenty-hour fund raising efforts on behalf of Muscular Dystrophy, Labor Day and Jerry Lewis will forever be entwined.

He made me laugh.

January 2017

Binghamton Provided Unforgettable Friendship (From the Binghamton Sun Bulletin, January 6, 2017)

In 1979, I had just started my first paying job in television news working for WICZ. I lived in Johnson City.

I knew no one other than my work colleagues. My girlfriend (who would later become my wife) lived nearly an hour away. I was a recent college graduate with the good fortune to land a great job just one week after getting my diploma from Syracuse University.

The advice from a professor was to get to know the community as quickly as possible. During the day, I met the newsmakers. After work, I walked around town trying to meet the people who were my audience.

That's when I met Andy. He was an elderly man who I would see crossing the street at a moderately busy intersection between my apartment and where he lived.

I saw him walking daily. I greeted him with a smile. Later encounters would be met with a wave and a small bit of conversation. "Nice weather we've been having?" I'd ask.

It wasn't long before he introduced himself.

"I'm Andy, my friend. What's your name?"

I introduced myself and started a friendship that would last the entire time I worked in Binghamton.

"Want to play checkers?" he asked.

Without giving it much thought, I said yes.

That began a weekly visit to where Andy stayed with his daughter and her husband just a few blocks from where I lived. We'd play for two hours, and then shake hands before leaving.

Our weekly games were not about the checkers. It was about bonding as friends. I'd share a story about a news interview I had done that week. He would tell the story about George Johnson. We had pleasant conversations over the checkerboard.

Soon, Andy taught me the game of chess. He would walk me through the basic moves and consistently win. His simple advice: "Always be thinking of the next move, the move after that, and the move after that one."

One night, I finally won. He offered his hand in congratulations with a big smile. After that, we generally split the number of games won.

I began working nights, so our games moved to afternoons. Soon, Andy was moved to a nursing home. I then paid my weekly visits to his new address right up until I left Binghamton for a new job in Alabama.

On that last afternoon we played chess, we both knew a special time was coming to an end. We parted with a handshake and, this time, a hug. He told me he thought of me like I was a son. I thanked him for taking that important first step of introducing himself to me. I left with tears in my eyes and gratitude for having this important first friend as I started my professional life. As I left his room that afternoon, I knew that I would probably never see him again.

In the late 1980s, I dropped by Andy's daughter's home. She wasn't in, but her husband told me how Andy had passed away peacefully in his sleep a couple of years after I left the community. Andy's daughter sent me a letter shortly after that visit to fill in some of the details, and to thank me for being his friend. She told me how he often spoke of our weekly chess games and that he truly cherished the time we'd spent talking to one another.

Families Really Matter

(Inspired by my book *Soft Skills for Hard Times*)

My mother Beatrice and me from the late 1970s.

If you want to make your mother happy, accomplish something.

I recently tried to answer the questions "when did I see Mom at her happiest?" There was the National Honor Society induction from high school that she kept as a secret from me so she could sneak in the back of the auditorium when my name was called.

There was my graduation from Herkimer College followed two years later by my graduation from Syracuse University.

She was very happy when she visited my wife and me in Hunstville while my wife was pregnant. She gathered several gifts from various family members and gave us a baby shower (a surprise, naturally) one-thousand miles from my hometown.

I think the night in the summer of 1979 when I anchored the news at WICZ-TV in Binghamton while my parents watched from my apartment might have the night she was the happiest. She and my dad came to Binghamton in the mid-evening just so they'd get a chance to see me on the air for that night's eleven o'clock news. They stopped by the station first to pick up my apartment key. Both were impressed as I gave them a brief tour of the television studio. I sent them on their way to my apartment so that they could see that night's newscast.

The newscast aired, and it was one of our better efforts. I rushed home to find both Mom and Dad proud and happy to see their son. All those years encouraging me to succeed in college, work hard, and do my best were finally paying off.

So I think it was that summer Friday night when my Mom got to see me read the news on local television was one of the nights where she was the happiest.

Or maybe, that was the night I was the happiest to be her son.

Photos

The WICZ, Channel 40 News Team in 1979. Top: Steve Newvine, Mark Williams (News Director), Sal Anthony. Bottom: Peg Donovan and Fred Heckman

My first friend in the Triple Cities, Andy.

News Director Mark Williams works the phones while I work on a story, typed out on a Smith Corona portable typewriter, for the Eyewitness News 6 PM edition.

Steve and Vaune Newvine on their wedding day.

Hosting the Jerry Lewis Labor Day Telethon in the wee hours of Labor Day in 1979 for WICZ-TV. The station did a twenty-hour remote broadcast at the Oakdale Mall in Johnson City.

On the back balcony of our first apartment in Owego, NY about 25 miles west of Binghamton. The apartment overlooked the Susquehana River.

I worked with Rick Krolak thirty years before that fatal helicopter crash in Phoenix. Rick and three other journalists were killed when two choppers crashed in mid-air while covering a news story.in the summer of 2007.
(Photo- WNEP)

From 1979, in the studio of WICZ-TV in Binghamton.

Speidies Marinade Recipe

4-5 lbs. cubed meat (chicken, pork, beef, or lamb)

1 Tablespoon salt

½ teaspoon pepper

¾ teaspoon oregano

1 tablespoon lemon juice

½ cup salad oil

1 cup wine vinegar

¼ to ½ cup water

¼ teaspoon sweet basil

3 cloves garlic, diced

Mix all ingredients together. Let stand for 48 hours. Turn occasionally. Barbecue the cubes on skewers and serve with fresh rolls.

(From the Recipes Remembers, the St. Agnes Cookbook, published in 1997, Avon, NY)

*Handwritten note by Vaune Newvine in our copy of the cookbook suggests adding minced onion to taste.

Stand By, Camera One is Steve Newvine's eleventh book. He writes the *Our Community Story column* twice monthly for the website: MercedCountyEvents.com. He has been honored with awards from Pacific Gas and Electric Company, Public Relations Society of America, and the Associated Press. He served as Chair of the Merced County Workforce Development Board, and in a number of community agencies. He lives in Merced, California with his wife Vaune.

Dear Readers:

Thanks for reading this book. I appreciate your support for my writing projects over the years.

Steve Newvine
SteveNewvine@sbcglobal.net